WHAT NOW, KNUCKLEHEAD?

WHAT NOW, KNUCKLEHEAD?

RAYMOND L. JONES

DEEDS PUBLISHING | ATLANTA

Published by Deeds Publishing, Marietta, GA
www.deedspublishing.com

Library of Congress Cataloging-in-Publications Data is available upon request.

ISBN 978-1-941165-49-2

Books are available in quantity for promotional or premium use. For information, write Deeds Publishing, PO Box 682212, Marietta, GA 30068 or info@deedspublishing.com.

10 9 8 7 6 5 4 3 2 1

CONTENTS

Part Two: Commission   105

Epilogue   187

Excerpt from We were Knuckleheads Once…And Always   211

I'd like to dedicate this book to all the knuckleheads I've met in my life. To name a few: Joseph Greer, for inspiring me to write this book; my wife and kids, just 'cause; and finally, Leo Cannon—yes, it is story time with CPT Jones.

ACKNOWLEDGMENTS

I STARTED THIS BOOK WHILE ON MY THIRD DEPLOYMENT IN IRAQ IN 2008. I was the night shift battle major working for 41st Fires Brigade on Forward Operating Base Delta, Al Kut, Iraq.

I have always been a story teller and I do like to laugh a lot. I tend to add or subtract a little from my stories in order to create a humorous outcome as I love to make others laugh as well. Life is full of enough bullshit so I figure you might as well enjoy the trip.

While on night shift in 2008, I discovered a new definition for boredom. If you think you've experienced dull, try sitting in an operations center with about a dozen or so other soldiers staring at a computer screen twelve hours a day, seven days a week. So, I figured why waste my time? I started writing on this book when nothing else was going on. With that confession, I'd like to offer thanks to all the Iraqis in and around Al Kut for not attacking the base or otherwise causing disruption. That allowed me to develop the initial skeleton for this book. I'll swear we had fewer significant activities[1] during that whole deployment (10 months) than I experienced during a week while in Tikrit, Iraq, in 2003 with 1-22 Infantry.

I was sitting in in the operations center one night when I got an Email from SSG Joseph Greer asking if I was the same Raymond Jones who was his platoon leader several years earlier. In fact I was. He and I started an email exchange that more or less ended with him asking if I had ever gotten around to writing the book I kept talking about "back in the day." I remembered I would walk around and point out silliness to others and exclaim I should write a book about all these "Knuckleheads."

---

1. Significant activities—Things that make you stop writing a book and focus your efforts elsewhere. You know, things like IEDs or roadside bombs, artillery or mortar attacks, snipers, etc.

That question from Joseph was the catalyst I needed to start writing. So, thanks, Joe. I've finally finished it!

Once back home, I put the book aside and started focusing on other stuff. From time to time I would pull out the manuscript, dust it off, and add some more stories. I had never heard of "self-publishing" nor did I have an inkling of how to get a book published. I more or less thought the book would end up being just digits on my computer and eventually lost to time.

Years later, on my fifth deployment, yet another truly dull time, I was working on III Corps Staff for Colonel Gary Brito. My job description was as an artillery subject matter expert. Although I am artillerist and I do understand the tactical level of the system, I had never worked on a Corps staff[2] and I was way out of my element. Colonel Brito could tell I was way out of my league and in a position I was under-qualified for. He did his level best to dumb things down to my level of understanding, yet I was too thick for most of his efforts. I'd like to acknowledge Colonel Gary Brito for not digging into my ass for working on my book instead of focusing on my work.

Around this time I discovered Amazon CreateSpace for self-publishing. I figured "What the hell?" I published my first book, *This Page Intentionally Left Blank, FM 101 Knuckleheads*.

Truthfully, that effort was a mitigated disaster. I don't blame Amazon as they did exactly what they advertised. I lacked the experience and know-how to effectively produce a quality product. Nonetheless, it was published and I sold close to a 100 books, both paperback and digital.

I had talked to Bob Babcock on the phone while in Iraq that third deployment and sought advice, which he gave freely. Then I forgot all about it. Years later, after I published that first book, I was frustrated with the lack of performance of the book. I felt like I was spinning my wheels and going nowhere. My wife suggested I call Bob Babcock, CEO of Deeds Publishing out of Atlanta, GA for assistance. Why didn't I think of that? I called Bob and he requested I send him a copy of the book, which I did. About a week later he called me back and suggested I re-work the book and publish it under a different title. He made some suggestions which I followed and I hope we have the start of a great relationship. I'd like to thank Bob for all his guidance and help.

---

2. For you civilians, when you think of Corps Level think "Corporate level" or echelons above reality.

Bob suggested Cecilia Stratton, former director of the 4th Infantry Division Museum at Fort Hood as the editor for my book. Although I have lived near Fort Hood for years I had never met Cecilia. I do look forward to meeting her someday and offer her a hug as thanks for all her efforts. Her suggestions only made the manuscript better.

There are tons of folks who have helped with the development of this manuscript. I apologize up front for anyone I left out. To name the ones I remember:

There's Dallice Jones (my wife) who puts up with my shit, why I don't know, regardless of its origin…(I'll let your imagination wonder)

Hank Jones (my brother) who is really good at pointing out my mistakes. He has been doing that for years so I figure with all that experience he must be right.

Tony Brooks (my cousin) helped me develop my webpage—a true genius.

Andrew White of Kilroy's Conversations, 1160 KVCE AM Radio, who, in spite of my dipshit efforts, is relentless in helping me promote my works.

Tim Ungaro who introduced me to Andrew White.

George Duncan of Barley and Hops, a home brew shop in Copperas Cove, Texas, for letting me chase Copperas Cove water with his outstanding home brew.

Leo Cannon, William Polumbo, Ryan Debeltz, and many others who have suffered through hours of listening to my stories and not punching me in the nose.

Finally, I'd like to acknowledge all those knuckleheads I've written about. Without your bumbles, fumbles, and troubles, I wouldn't have anything to laugh about, nor write about. Keep it up!

INTRODUCTION

IN MY TWENTY SOME ODD YEARS OF MILITARY SERVICE, I RAN INTO ALL sorts of characters from all over the world and all walks of life. I feel honored to have known most of the people I met. If you want facts, talk to a lawyer; if you want truth, talk to a philosopher. The stories in this book are neither facts (although most myths are rooted in facts), nor are they truths (as truth is in the eye of the beholder). Here we have "mystory," not history. My intent is to entertain, educate (loosely), or illuminate folks as to what may have been.

All people, at one point or another, are knuckleheads. The key to a successful life is to enjoy the trip, not fret about the destination. If one can't laugh at oneself, then he or she has no right to laugh at others. I constantly poke fun at myself. My father would agree that I'm one of the biggest knuckleheads walking around, so I make it a goal to point out the funny things others do. One thing to remember about "soldier stories" is that a soldier is a hero in every story he tells. No soldier ever starts his story by saying, "I'm the dirtbag who did this or that."

My uncle, Mark, was fond of telling whoppers when he was just a child. When someone questioned one of his stories, he'd simply say, "That how it's done in the Malpais."* Where he got this saying is a mystery among my immediate family.

My grandfather was a grand storyteller. He'd tell tales that made most people bust a gut, pull something, or pee themselves with laughter. What I'm trying to say is that I come by my ability to embellish naturally. We learn through telling stories. If the story doesn't match the situation, change the story. The point is always there.

I've left out the names of the innocent (or the guilty, depending on how one reads the stories) in an effort to keep these stories innocent and humorous. I hope you enjoy this book, and I hope it makes you think of all the knuckleheads you've met during your life.

*The Malpais is a lava formation near our old family ranch in New Mexico.

PART ONE
ENLISTMENT

THE M60 AND THE CHECK POINT

WHEN I FIRST ENLISTED, I ENLISTED IN THE TEXAS ARMY NATIONAL GUARD. I was 17 and a junior, still in high school. I guess the reason I joined was because of my older brother. Now my brother isn't in the military and is, in fact, what I like to refer to as a Texas Hippie. He is a college professor at a small college in Central Texas where he preaches peace and is a big advocate of anti-war with non-violent resolution…that is at least until you piss him off. Then he'll kick your ass. Believe me, I have been on the receiving end of those ass kickin's and it ain't fun! So, how did this Texas Hippie inspire me to join up?

Well, that has to do with money. See, when I was 17 and my brother 19, I was living at home and he was going to school in Austin, Texas. I saw how expensive it was for my parents to put one kid through college and the sacrifices they were making. My father was recently retired from the army still trying to figure out what he wanted to do with the rest of his life and my mother was working as a teacher in our local school. Money wasn't exactly pouring into our family bank account. Truthfully, funds were rather scarce during this time period of the Jones family. We weren't exactly poor but every little bit counted. I didn't want to be a further burden on them so I decided to take matters into my own hands and signed up. The National Guard, at that time, was offering some pretty good incentives and had a small stipend for those going to college. It didn't pay outright for college, it just helped a little. Besides, by joining up, I got the chance to head off one weekend a month and play soldier. Lots of fun.

I enlisted as a mechanic. I have always been enthralled by the workings and insides of machines. I have always liked tearing things apart just to see if I could put it back together. The National Guard armory near my home town had a vacancy for a mechanic and so I thought, "What the hell? I'll join up, earn a little extra cash, get to shoot a rifle or a machine gun from time to time—and get paid to do so!" Again, lots of fun.

Before my initial entry training (or basic training as it is more commonly known) I did all the normal high school things you know—chase girls, drink beer, try to cause as much trouble as I could, and not get caught. Not easy in a small town where everyone knows your father. But I did my damnedest.

From time to time, one weekend a month to be precise, I would have to go to guard drills. I was just a 17 year old private at the time so I did a lot more watching, cleaning and go-fering (you know, go-fer this and go-fer that) than I did actual mechanic work; but I was getting paid and doing some fun stuff on the side.

One weekend my guard unit was supposed to qualify on the M60 machine gun. Now, if you have never fired an M60, then I recommend you do when and if you get the chance. In my opinion, it's life altering having that kind of power at your fingertips. The company I was assigned to was in one town and the battalion was in another town about forty miles up the road. In the town where the battalion headquarters was located there was a training area that included a range where we could shoot our machine guns. So, we loaded the weapons (and a couple of cases of beer as some national guard units were wont to do in those days) in the back of a deuce and a half truck and headed on up to the range complex.

A little bit down the road, the local sheriff's department had decided to set up a check point with the intent of catching drunk drivers. As the deuce and a half came barreling down the hill towards the check point, one of the fellas in the back with the machine guns decided it would be a good idea to load one of the guns with some blank ammunition. He yelled at the driver to speed up as he pulled the trigger. The check point erupted in complete chaos as we blasted our way down the road and past the check point.

Now, remember the part where I said I was a 17 year old private? Well, I was scared shitless by all this. I thought for sure we were all going to jail and I'd have to call my father to bail me out. I saw one of the sheriff's deputies jump into his cruiser, flip his whoopee lights on, and begin to chase after us. About a half mile down the road the guy driving the truck pulled over and the deputy—at first at least—was pissed as hell. That was until he saw who had fired the machine gun. Apparently the deputy and the machine gunner were brothers.

I could tell the deputy was still a little ticked, but as all the other guys were falling over themselves laughing their asses off, I guess the deputy decided we didn't need a trip to the jail house so he let us go. We eventually made it to the range where we must have shot 10,000 rounds. Lots of fun…

LT BEETLE BAILEY

MY FIRST SUPERVISOR IN THE ARMY WAS A STAFF SERGEANT WE ALL AFFEC-tionately called "Dutch." Dutch was about 6 feet tall, weighed maybe 220 pounds or so, and was rather stocky. To be completely honest, he had arms the size of bowling balls and a beer barrel chest to match. This guy truly impressed me by his sheer strength. He was the type of guy who could drop a transmission onto his chest, crawl out from underneath the vehicle, and fix the transmission. Then, he could crawl back under the vehicle and hold the transmission in place with one arm while bolting it in place with the other one. For the most part he seemed to be a pretty nice fella, knowledgeable about his skill, and pretty experienced about life in general.

As stated earlier, I was still pretty new to this whole "army thing." I mean, my father had been in the army, not me. I knew a little about protocol, customs and courtesies, and general military things, but I really didn't know what it was like being a soldier. I had yet to go off to basic training but since I had enlisted I was required to attend drill and just generally stay out of everybody's way as I was "untrained" at everything. They let me clean things up or take out the garbage and other little things, but by and large, I was just watching and learning.

High Mobility Multipurpose Wheeled Vehicle (HMMWVs or Hummers) were just being introduced to the military and our guard unit had one or two for us to train on. We mostly used the old GPVs (or General Purpose Vehicles, also known as jeeps) for getting around. I personally think the army made a big mistake going away from these small maintenance-friendly, utility vehicles. They were easy to fix, hard to get stuck in the mud, and for the most part they were fuel efficient, being so light and only having a four cylinder engine. Maybe the army could have just upgraded them rather than coming out with a new vehicle.

To demonstrate how good Dutch was at his chosen profession, I remember one time Dutch and I were driving around in one of those old jeeps when all of a sudden the engine decided to die on us. Dutch climbed out of the driver's seat and popped the hood in order to take a look see as to the cause of the engine dying. He pulled the Leatherman (a multi-tool about the size of a pocket knife) and popped the carburetor off the top of the engine. He proceeded to clean the carburetor and then replaced it back on the engine. The jeep fired right up and away we went. After years of working on HMMWV's, I never was able to repair an engine malfunction with just a Leatherman and a little know-how. The vehicles the army has now are not at all "mechanic friendly" and require folks specialized in the repair of specific parts of each vehicle. No one mechanic is charged with working on the whole vehicle. It's a shame we've gone with these new vehicles...back to the story.

This particular drill weekend we were supposed to do drivers training on this new HMMWV and all of us were supposed to get licensed on its operation. So, Dutch took all of us out and showed us how to conduct the operator level maintenance, the start-up procedures, and operation in extreme conditions procedures (how to drive it through the mud in other words). He finished the class by saying, "It's nearly impossible to get this vehicle stuck." Famous last words I suppose.

We took the HMMWV out for our test drive. Several of the other soldiers in the vehicle were in line to drive before me so I just sat in the back and more or less observed how they drove. I nodded off a time or two 'cause it was a hot day and it's generally boring watching someone else drive. Finally it was my turn to drive. I climbed into the driver's seat and took off like a bat out of hell. I was young and rather inexperienced (when compared to some) about the ins and outs of four wheeling.

Off to my left I saw a large mound of dirt. Remembering Dutch's word's "*It's nearly impossible to get this vehicle stuck*," I decided I was going up and over that mound. I lined the vehicle up and punched the throttle. If you haven't guessed yet, I got the vehicle stuck. Dutch, God bless him, looked at me and said, "You're digging it out."

With that, I spent the next three or four hours digging with the little shovel that was part of the pioneer kit[3]. Afterwards, Dutch pulled me aside and told me the bad news. Because I had gotten the vehicle stuck, I would still be labeled as "untrained" on the HMMWV. I would have my chance at a later date to try again. Just not today. I had already made

3. A little kit tucked up under the rear part of the vehicle; it contains a shovel, mattocks pick with handle, and other little useful tools

him late for a meeting and with that, he climbed back into the driver's seat and we headed back to the maintenance building.

When we got back it seemed the meeting I had made Dutch late for must have been rather important because the motor officer was mad as hell at Dutch. Dutch tried to explain what had happened, but for some reason the motor officer wasn't having any of the excuse. Dutch backed-off the lieutenant, putting his hands up in a defensive position saying, "Hey sir, I don't know what your beef is but I don't want none of it." Dutch tried to walk around the lieutenant but the lieutenant stepped in front of him. Dutch accidently bumped into the lieutenant and before he could get out an "I'm sorry," the lieutenant said, "HEY, you just assaulted an officer, I'm gonna make you pay for that!"

Mind you, I thought all this was my fault because I had gotten the vehicle stuck on that dirt mound. I started to step forward so as to intervene when one of the other guys reached out and grabbed my shoulder, telling me to stay out of it. Apparently, the lieutenant had at one time dated Dutch's daughter (this was the National Guard after all, we mostly all lived near one another) and she dumped him for another guy. When the lieutenant had gone to Dutch for assistance in getting her back, Dutch told the lieutenant that he made it a rule to not mix National Guard things and personal things. Basically Dutch told him, "You're on your own, buddy." This didn't set too well with the lieutenant. All this had occurred months earlier and the lieutenant had been looking for a reason to get at Dutch since.

Anyway, Dutch looked at the lieutenant and asked, "What do you mean by, 'I'm gonna make you pay'?"

"I think you know what I mean. You assaulted a superior officer. I'm gonna see that you get court-martialed!"

"Well then, I might as well get my money's worth," Dutch replied.

With that, Dutch landed the most perfect uppercut I have ever seen right to the end of the lieutenant's chin. I have seen dozens of guys hit with uppercuts but, I have never seen a guy's feet leave the ground (other than in the movies). I swear, the lieutenant must have been airborne a clear two feet off the ground. When he landed, he was out cold. With the lieutenant lying there on the ground and Dutch standing over him, it looked just like Mort Walker's *Beetle Bailey*, with Beetle lying on the ground with X's over his eyes and big Sarge standing over him.

As far as I know, nothing happened to Dutch for this little altercation. I mean afterwards he was still a Staff Sergeant and still my supervisor.

I'm sure someone had a little talk with him about his aggressive behavior towards the lieutenant, but other than that nothing visible to us subordinates.

The lieutenant on the other hand, well, he was transferred out of the motor pool and a few weeks later out of the unit.

THE NEUTRAL ZONE

4 JUNE 1989, I CLIMBED ABOARD A BUS THAT TOOK ME TO THE MILITARY Entrance Processing Station (MEPS). MEPS is used by the army for a couple of different reasons. It's where most enlisted folks go to get their first physical, to get sworn in, and (at least in my case) where I went to get my plane ticket to go to basic training.

You meet all kinds of folks at MEPS. The NCOs there more or less segregate the enlistees so there isn't much fraternization between those going to basic training and those there for other purposes. Being a 17 year old in a man's world, I did my level best to look as old as possible as well as act like a man. I think just about everybody does.

I remember there was this one kid, maybe a year or so older than me, who was from Killeen, Texas (near Fort Hood). I think his father had been in the army. He kept on trying to tell me how much he knew about being in the army. I listened out of politeness but truthfully, I knew he was a blow hard. Incidentally, he and I ended up in the same platoon at basic and it turned out he didn't know as much as he thought he did. All in all, I think there were fifteen to twenty of us at the MEPS station en route to basic training.

Early in the morning on 5 June, we boarded a plane that took us to Missouri, with Fort Leonard Wood being our final destination. We climbed off the plane and were met by a military liaison that organized us and put us on another bus headed to the post.

Our first billeting on Fort Leonard Wood looked to be World War II era buildings called the Neutral Zone, also known as the "In Processing Center." The billets at the Neutral Zone smelled of rotten wood and the walls were in a bad need of paint. The intent of this stop was to in-process us for basic training and to wait until they had enough trainees to make up a class. Folks were flying in from everywhere. This took about three days. One thing of note, I'm sure most of you know what happens when you take fellas from all over the US and shove them into a room together.

If you don't, I'm here to tell you; you get sick. Most common is the upper respiratory infection from all those little buggies from the distant locations of the country. Kind of a rough time.

Anyways, one of the first things we were to receive was all of our shots followed by our uniforms, and then we had to pass a physical fitness test. Now, this test wasn't anything like the Army Physical Fitness Test (APFT). This was just to make sure a guy had enough upper body strength to make it through the initial entry phase of basic training. If my memory serves me right, you had to be able to complete thirteen proper push-ups. I passed mine with flying colors. Some of the others weren't so lucky.

I sometimes get perturbed when I hear folks my age now talk about how "unhealthy" and "unfit" kids are today as if "back in the day" we had it all figured out. Truth is; there have always been roly-polies—my generation notwithstanding. I think there were about a dozen or so trainees of the sixty plus trainees going through the Neutral Zone who couldn't pass the test. They were off to what was known as Charlie's Fat Farm or CFF. There they conducted physical fitness three or four times a day until they were able to pass the test. At that point they were allowed to join whatever cycle was next in the hopper.

Going through the uniform issuing warehouse is probably as close to a manufacturing assembly line a human being will ever come to. You enter the one end looking like a ragtag civilian and pop out the other with our heads clean shaven, arms sore from the shots, and wearing brand new uniforms. We're given one of those green duffle bags and that is where we were supposed to place our unused uniforms and other issue items, as well as the civilian clothes we arrived in. Looking back, I was amazed at how difficult it was for me to fit all that stuff in that duffle bag. Today? Well, today I can get about twice to three times as much stuff in a duffle bag than I could in those days. As a side note, my best time for packing my deployment bag is about two minutes thirty-two seconds— that includes a "to standard" inventory list…Just saying.

At the end of this day we were at least more or less looking like soldiers. There was still eight weeks ahead of us. The next morning our world would be rocked.

DRILL SERGEANTS DO HAVE A SENSE OF HUMOR

EARLY IN THE MORNING WE WOKE UP AND ATE BREAKFAST. THERE WAS AN odd, eerie feeling because folks were being downright nice to us. A day earlier when going through the chow hall the servers were rather stingy with the portions, but this day? They were passing out heaping mounds of food. I would discover why later.

We finished chow, grabbed our duffle bags, and stood in line waiting for what we would affectionately call "cattle cars." Now, if you've never seen a real cattle car just come down to Texas and you'll see what we're talking about. In Texas, a cattle car is a semi attached to a trailer where we pack cows in so tight there isn't enough room for them to move. On the surface this might sound cruel; in reality, well, we pack them so tight so they don't end up kicking each other to death while the vehicle is moving. For you vegetarians out there who think eating meat is a violation of some natural order or a sin of sorts, well, all I have to say to you is, plants are alive, too.

The cattle cars we rode are so named because we are crammed into the cargo area much like the cattle are in actual cattle cars. In the front of the car our drill sergeant sat with his famed "brown and round" hat sitting on his head. I swear, to this day that man epitomized what perfection means to me. He looked so professional. I mean, truthfully, over the past couple of days all of us trainees had passed stories around—true or otherwise—about how scary these drill sergeants were. I believe I was truly afraid.

However, as we drove around post en route to our barracks, the drill sergeant would occasionally turn around and point out areas of interest to us. I mean, this felt more like an uncomfortable tour guide than it did a military operation. He pointed out the swimming pool, the bowling alley, and the parade field where he said, "The girls come out here on Saturday to watch the guys play flag football." This was not at all what I was expecting. Maybe all those stories about evil drill sergeants were just hype?

As we arrived at the barracks, the drill sergeant climbed out of the front and walked around to the door where we would exit. The driver opened the door and the drill sergeant spoke in a calm and cool voice.

"Now, this is the place where you will call home for the next eight weeks. It's our job to ensure you have a memorable experience with us here at Fort Leonard Wood. Once you exit the bus I want you to find the fella's out here who have bars on their hats. These guys are the bell hops and they will take your duffle bags to your room. Just drop the bag at their feet then line up in formation and we'll get started, ok?"

He looked around a bit in order to eyeball every one of us. He started off in a soft voice,

"Now, you have exactly one minute to get off my cattle car, AND THIRTY SECONDS ARE ALREADY GONE!!! NOW MOVE!!"

Now, like I said earlier, I was raised an army brat so I more or less knew the different ranks and their structure so I didn't fall for the drill sergeant's little ploy. One of the other guys wasn't so lucky. As soon as this other fella left the bus he heaved his duffle bag in the direction of the first lieutenant he saw, hitting that lieutenant square in the gut with the duffle bag. If it weren't so tragic, what happened to him afterward, I think I would've laughed my ass off. The lieutenant picked himself off the ground, his face beet red; one of the other drill sergeants took that kid off to the side and gave him some personal attention. Now, I did play football in Texas. The training we did for football didn't even compare to the calisthenics they made that poor kid do. Poor unfortunate soul.

That day is burned into my mind. I will never forget meeting our drill sergeants for the first time. By the way, I figured out why those chow hall folks at the Neutral Zone had been so generous with the portions. We all got to taste that chow a second time as we puked our guts out doing the infamous duffle bag shuffle. If you have to ask what that is, you don't want to know.

Sadistic is all that comes to mind.

THE GAS CHAMBER

ONE OF THE MORE MEMORABLE EXPERIENCES ONE WILL HAVE WHILE AT-
tending basic training has to be the gas chamber. This is a horrific experience. If you've been fortunate enough to not find yourself in an enclosed
chamber with tons of CS gas, count your blessings. If you have, well
then, "I feel your pain, brother."

Truthfully, it's not as bad as all that, but that first time in the chamber
does make you thank your lucky stars you weren't a part of the holocaust
and that Hitler was put down. CS gas is bad enough. I don't ever want
to even think of those trenches in World War I. All that gas. Must have
been truly horrible…

At any rate, the reason the gas chamber is part of basic training
has everything to do with World War I and those trenches. Chemical
and Biological weaponry is sometimes referred to as "the poor man's
nuclear weapon" 'cause they are cheap to make and devastating in their
effectiveness. I do believe these types of weapons need to continue to be
outlawed—especially when used against the US. If our enemies want to
use them on each other, well, I suppose that's ok…(my little plug into
politics).

The whole point of going through the gas chamber is to give the new
soldier the confidence his equipment works. While in the chamber you
normally have to remove the mask and say something like, the platoon
motto or the last four of your social security number, or something else
where at least you have to take a breath of that gas. Then you are supposed
to clear and reseal the mask and exit the chamber.

Once outside the chamber you trot around in a circle, coughing,
wheezing, blowing snot on yourself, and in some cases puking your
last meal up. I am sure this is cause for great amusement amongst those
sadistic drill sergeants standing around "supervising" the whole ordeal.
We did our chamber right after our lunch meal. The drill sergeant jogged
us out to the chamber—about a two mile jog—so as to get us all nice and

sweaty so the gas would penetrate the pores on our skin, causing more irritation. I'm sure he thought he was doing us a favor. Not sure I agree with his logic but, it is what it is.

I remember this one kid, also from Texas I'm sorry to say, well, he must have been claustrophobic because as soon as he was shut into that chamber he freaked the hell out. The soldier charged the exit door with enough force to knock it open and run over the drill sergeant who was standing there. He then proceeded to run off into the tree line with no less than three drill sergeants chasing after him. The drill sergeants soon overtook him and commenced to really beat him down. Once most of the fight was out of the soldier, the drill sergeants picked him up and carried him back over to the chamber, pitched him in (without his mask), and then shut the door. They left him in there for a good five minutes or so before dragging him out. After a few minutes of him writhing on the ground he eventually sat up and regained some of his faculties. Abusive? I suppose. Years later, upon reflection, I'm certain these drill sergeants broke at least a dozen or so regulations or policies, but when you're a seventeen year old kid watching all this unfold you just figure it's part of army life.

I mean one could take several schools of thought on the subject. Truthfully, the kid did assault a drill sergeant by barreling over him when the soldier blew through the door. He did need to be shown that the CS gas wasn't going to kill him and that his equipment does function properly. But there may have been a less aggressive means to accomplish this. Basically, one could consider this kid just a wimp and he needed to either man up or get the hell out; on the other hand, the drill sergeants probably didn't need to beat him down nor throw him into to the gas chamber for five minutes. I don't know what happened to that kid after that.

On a good note, after one is finished with the gas chamber, any remnants of the upper respiratory infection are gone. The gas causes a guy to cough up a lung...I swear.

BRM

FOR THE NEXT THREE WEEKS WE WENT THROUGH WHAT WAS KNOWN AS Basic Rifleman Marksmanship (BRM) and I was introduced to the M16 rifle for the first time in my life. I mean, as stated earlier, my dad was in the army and I knew they had these M16 type rifles, and I had seen them before, but my father didn't bring his home. To dismiss any thoughts to the contrary, the army's sensitivity to the accounting of its weapons is sacred. Ask anyone who's been "dress right dress" walking across an open range looking for a "sensitive" item like an M16. All training (and what seems like the whole world) comes to a screeching halt if a weapon is lost or unaccounted for. This concept is engrained in the new private at basic training.

Anyway, this BRM training we went through was pretty basic (I mean after all it is "basic training"). First we started off with how to break the weapon down and put it back together, how and why to clean it, and then we got into how to shoot it. If you've never used the sights on an M16, it might be hard to imagine, but they really are pretty easy to use and can be adjusted for just about anyone to use effectively.

We did all the "non" firing training first, then headed out to the range and put our first rounds down range through this rifle. I must admit I didn't do so well at the beginning of this training. I had been brought up on traditional rifles and sights so these were a new concept with me. After I was able to shoot several rounds through the rifle I got better. For any gun control freaks, it doesn't matter what the stock looks like—a traditional stock, an assault stock, or even a bull pup stock—the rifle is the dangerous part. Additionally, if guns were the cause of all the problems in the world then we would have lots of problems in the army, especially during basic...but we don't. It's the asshole behind the gun causing the problem (...another political statement—maybe I should run for office?)

At the end of three weeks we finished up our BRM training and one might think that afterwards we would turn our weapons in and be done with it. However, the army wants its soldiers to get used to carrying the rifle everywhere we go, so we pretty much signed them out just about every day. This is where the knucklehead stories come in...

I have actually seen one of my battle buddies drop his rifle into a port-a-potty. For some dumb reason he rested the weapon up next to him as he did his business. After he was done, he stood up and bumped the rifle, and after a little moment of panic, "plop", there it went. He really didn't know what to do so he went back to his squad without the rifle. The drill sergeant dug into him almost right away. Next thing I knew a couple of others and I had to hold onto his boots as he head dove into the port-a-john with the intent of pulling his rifle out. Talk about your awkward situations. His rifle never did smell quite right after that. Come to think about it, neither did he.

ABERDEEN PROVING GROUNDS

RIGHT AFTER BASIC TRAINING I WAS SENT HOME. AT THE TIME I WAS WHAT is referred to as a "split-op" or split option, which meant I would do basic training the summer between my junior and senior years of high school and then head back for Advanced Individual Training (AIT) the next summer. The split option was perfect for me as I was still in high school. AIT is where a soldier learns his job skills. I was to be a tracked vehicle repairer and that school is located in Aberdeen Proving Grounds, Edgewood Arsenal, in Maryland.

The trip to AIT was a bit different than the trip to basic training; first off, I more or less knew what was expected of me; and secondly, well there were going to be females in our class. Now, for you women libists (is this a word or does it even matter?) out there, this was 1990, and although women have served in one fashion or another since 1775, they had only been integrated into the mainstream army since 1978. We're talking only twelve years here. There were still a bunch of hold outs who didn't think men and women serving side by side was acceptable.

During times of change, the current generation always has the hardest time living with the change. With every generation after the change, things get a little easier as the change becomes the social norm. One could argue I was part of the second generation of this change. I personally didn't see any problem with females integrated into male units. Now, decades later —especially after the gulf wars—women have proven this bias as false. So, don't judge these hold outs too harshly. They're only doing what comes naturally to them. On the other hand, there are some hold outs using their positions as leverage and abuse the trust given to them as leaders in order to satisfy some lustful desires. These folks have a "rotten to the core" sickness and have more than likely abused their authority in the past as this type of behavior doesn't manifest itself overnight. It's been there all along.

Case in point, while at AIT in Aberdeen, we had a drill sergeant caught snooping around the female barracks peeking in the windows, trying to cop a gander at the females as they were changing their clothes. Apparently, when called out about this type of behavior, he tried to utilize his position as a drill sergeant, claiming he was just inspecting the security around the facility. He wasn't around much longer after that. I don't know what happened to him, as they don't tell privates that kind of information, but I assume they just transferred him to another "all-male" unit.

OOZING OUT OF THE GROUND

ONE INTERESTING FACT ABOUT ABERDEEN PROVING GROUNDS, EDGEWOOD Arsenal is that it has long been used as a testing ground for chemical warfare. It started right about the time of America's involvement in World War I and probably continues to this day. It has long been known that tons of chemical munitions and other toxic paraphernalia are buried all over the arsenal's 13,000 acres and from time to time those toxins seep to the surface and have to be dealt with.

During AIT at Edgewood Arsenal, the training lasted for thirteen weeks for tracked vehicle repairers like me. The first three weeks we were under what was known as "total control." This was meant to be a transition from basic training to a less controlling environment. If one passed the "gateway" inspection at the end of our third week we were given leniency, our civilian clothes, and allowed to have off post privileges on the weekends.

On this particular weekend, a couple of friends and I had decided to share a cab ride and head into town to watch a movie at one of the local theaters. I think we went to see Arnold Schwarzenegger's *Total Recall*, as it was just released that summer. After the movie, the other two guys hooked up with some of the local talent and were invited back to "party."

Now, I am sure I was invited but I had the feeling this party was going to be something I really didn't want any part of. I just had this gut feeling something was out of the ordinary so I opted to not go. It turned out I made a wise decision because both of my buddies ended up drunk. Since one was underage, well, the army doesn't like alcohol-related incidents. I'm not trying to say I'm a saint or anything. I have done my share of underage drinking. It's just that when it comes to the army I don't like to jack around with its policies or rules—especially when it comes to things like drinking or drugs. My opinion? The juice isn't worth the squeeze.

You might get away with it a hundred times but eventually you'll get caught. Every time you get away with it, it emboldens you to try it again. It's better to just never start.

As I was just a private and I had more time than money at this juncture, I decided to walk back to the billets. It wasn't more than five miles and I thought I could take a detour through the woods and shave a mile or so. So, I started to walk. I never make it a habit to make two wise decisions back to back, that's just a waste of good decisions. The decision to not go to the party…Good; the one to cut through the woods…Bad!

I started back along some of the main routes walking on the sidewalks until I got to the turnoff for the post. I had seen maps of the area and knew pretty much which direction was north, so I just went for it. I must have gotten about a half mile or so into the tree line when I ran across some yellow caution tape. Not feeling very cautious at the time I ignored the tape and continued through the wood line. Every now and then I caught a whiff of what I thought was chlorine. As strange as that sounds, in the middle of a wood line, I figured there was a laundromat nearby so I didn't think anything of it. I made it to the barracks and since it was getting on into the evening I settled down and went to sleep.

The next day was Sunday and as was the policy, all the trainees were to line up in formation for accountability. That's when I heard about my buddies getting drunk at the party. Apparently, one of the girl's parents didn't take too kindly to my buddy trying to get fresh with his daughter. I am pretty sure she was of age, but you can't be too sure about things like that. One of my other buddies asked how I made it home and when I told him about my walk through the woods, he kinda turned a little white and said, "You dipshit! You didn't read the warning in the in-processing packet! You walked through a munitions dump! A runner not too long ago was running through that area and came upon a herd of dead deer! There are tons of old World War I chemicals buried out there! You walked right through it!"

"I thought I smelled some chorine out there. I thought that was a bit strange since there weren't any laundromats nearby," was all I could say.

I never did get checked out. I was too afraid of getting into trouble for not reading the warnings in the packet. I never felt any ill effects so I just kept my mouth shut about it. Maybe I was just on the outskirts of the dump and the concentration of toxins wasn't too high. Who knows? Maybe God does love the ignorant.

THE TRIP HOME

AT THE END OF THE SUMMER, NEAR THE END OF AUGUST, WAS OUR GRADUATION. There were only five other tracked mechanics in my class as the rest of those in my platoon were heavy wheeled mechanics. Their AIT lasted sixteen weeks, so it was a smallish graduation to say the least. I had flown to Maryland at the beginning of the summer. Normally when a soldier flies one way they fly back as well. Earlier I mentioned I was an army brat, truth is my father was a retired army officer. As an enlisted guy I wanted to keep the "my dad's an officer" quiet as there are those NCOs who like to pick on guys like me, but now that I am a retired officer myself I guess it really doesn't matter anymore. So, my dad was a retired army officer and our last assignment had been overseas in Japan. He worked with the US Embassy and his job had something to do with goods being traded between our two countries.

At any rate, some of the kids my brother and I went to school with in Japan had recently returned and were scattered up and down the east coast. As I was getting ready to graduate from AIT I called my brother and asked him if he wanted to take this opportunity and visit some of our friends. I had money in the bank to blow and all I needed was a vehicle to get around. He agreed to make the trip and said he would be at my graduation. Remember how I said in that first story about my brother being a "Texas Hippie?" Now, don't misunderstand me, he loves the military and has always been my biggest supporter. He would give the shirt off his back to help out a soldier. He just believes conflict resolution needs to be handled by non-violent means before you pull out your guns. Me? I'm a "shoot first—ask questions later" kinda guy. Together we make up about the perfect combination. He is the yin to my yang.

So, he made the trip from Texas to Aberdeen in less than twenty-four hours. Now that may not sound very quick by today's standards, but remember, the speed limit in most areas in 1990 was still 55 mph. By my math, it should have taken him about twenty-six hours to make that trip.

He didn't stop unless he needed gas and he may have bumped his speed up a little bit from time to time (shhh!). Anyways, he made the trip and showed up about a day before my graduation.

When he made it to post he found his way to the training room for my company. You should have heard the shit storm that was raised because his hair was halfway down his back. The drill sergeants thought he was a National Guard trainee showing up for the next cycle. At first they gave him a ton of shit about his hair until they realized he wasn't there for training. I remember it pretty clear when a drill sergeant called down the hall in the barracks, "Jones! Jones! Jesus Christ is here to see you!"

My brother and I were able to spend the rest of the afternoon together and did quite a bit of catching up. Years later I realize that thirteen weeks really isn't all that long, but when you are an eighteen year old, it's an eternity. I discovered mom and dad were doing well. He also brought news that a couple of friends of mine had been in a wreck and one was dead. The others had been severely injured but were going to recover. I felt lucky to have been at AIT that summer. More than likely I would have been with my friends and might have been killed as well. The way life unweaves has always amazed me.

The next day was graduation and as there was only five of us it lasted about thirty minutes or so. By that afternoon my brother and I were on our way to New York to visit one of my old girl-friends. We really didn't know where we were going and as GPS had yet to make an appearance to us mainstream folks, we did a lot of "U" turns. Being a couple of country bumpkins driving around in a huge city we must have hit just about every cliché you can think of. We finally found the community where she lived, right around two a.m. We didn't want to disturb her family so we decided to pull the truck into a playground near where they lived. We planned to wait until daylight to knock on the door. We didn't have cell phones so there was no calling or texting before we showed up in those days. You just showed up.

Anyway, the decision to hole up and wait till morning turned out to be a foolish one. My brother and I fell asleep and were awakened a couple of hours later to a flashlight rapping on the window of the truck. Now, all I had ever heard about New York was the amount of gang activity that goes on there. To say the least, I was panicked. Looking at my brother I could see he wasn't too happy about these happenings either. I ensured the door was locked and began searching for something to defend myself. All of a sudden a policeman's badge was shoved up against the window.

It took a moment or two for me to gain my bearings, but eventually I opened the door and was manhandled against the hood of the truck and frisked. I saw my brother on the other side of the vehicle going through an experience about the same as mine.

"What are you doing here?" the cop asked.

"We were sleeping," was the only answer I could come up with.

"We're going to search your truck here, any issues?"

"Ah, no, not really. What's going on?" My brother asked.

Apparently, there had been a series of break-ins in that neighborhood and the cops were on alert for anything suspicious. I guess two fella's with out-of-state tags, sleeping in a playground, is suspicious. After a search of our truck they found a hatchet and a couple of bow saws.

"What do you use these for?"

"We're from Texas, we work on a family ranch and we use those from time to time."

"What are you doing in New York?"

I explained about being friends with one of the local girls and how we took this opportunity to visit. They followed us down to the girl's house and knocked on the door. Fortunately, her parents vouched for us and we didn't have to spend the night in a jail cell. Those cops did keep our tools after all. I guess they needed them more than we did.

We spent a couple of days there then decided to head up to Connecticut to visit one of my brother's friends. This is when I discovered that folks on the east coast cross state lines more often than we Texan's cross county lines. That's right; some of our counties are larger than their states! I never knew that before.

Texas lies in what is known to us as the "Bible belt." I guess that refers to the fact that you can't swing a dead cat without hitting a church in our neck of the woods. One of the issues with living in the Bible belt is that some counties are still dry. A dry county for you northern folks out there means there is no alcohol sold within the county's borders. You have to find a wet county to buy alcohol. As a side note, the dry counties in Texas are as dry as a martini and we have the alcoholics to prove it! These folks are known as backdoor Baptists, meaning, they drink all night with their friends then they sneak in the backdoor of the church on Sunday morning.

Anyways, our county in Texas is a dry county. We had to drive about thirty to forty-five miles to a different town in a different county to buy our liquor. I told you earlier that I didn't believe in drinking while under the shroud of the army. Well, now I was on my own and was willing to imbibe.

So, when we met up with my brother's friend we expected him to have at least some beer but were disappointed to find him fresh out. This was a problem, it was after midnight and apparently Connecticut doesn't sell alcohol after nine p.m. on a Saturday night till after noon on Sunday. New York's laws limit the sale after midnight; however, in New Jersey the laws vary by location. At any rate, he told us not to worry, he knew about a place where we could just pop over and buy our fill in New Jersey, about forty minutes away. I thought, holy shit, we'd be driving across two states' lines!

Now, about buying the alcohol, well, my brother was only twenty, his friend, twenty, and me, like I said, eighteen. Who was going to buy the alcohol? Well, it was me. I have been buying booze since I was thirteen. You see, I have been shaving since I was twelve and have had a full beard by the time I was thirteen. I was everyone's best friend on Friday night. So, all I really had to do was not shave for a couple of days, walk right in, and buy the booze. No real issue. We drove to New Jersey, bought some beer, then headed back to his place and relaxed.

My brother and I drove around for about another week or so visiting a few other friends without much incident. I had squirreled about $400 in the glove box—the amount I deemed needed for our return trip, so when we ran out of money we would have enough to drive home. The money I had in the bank sure didn't last as long as I thought it should have. I guess it never does.

I'M THE NCOUC

THE NEXT SUMMER I WAS STILL IN THE NATIONAL GUARD, AND AS THE guard does we were called to active duty for our two weeks in the summer (which is more like fifteen days). I had been through Basic Training and AIT so I was a certified mechanic and had a lot less go-ferring going on. They actually gave me a tool box and let me work on stuff. At nineteen I was in hog heaven. Desert Shield/Desert Storm had ended a few months earlier and there was a real concern there for a while that my unit could've been called to active duty in support of the campaign. Fortunately, Saddam's defensive plan and the effectiveness of our military eliminated that necessity. So life continued on for this young Texan.

Our two week excursion was to take place on Fort Hood, Texas. This was my first introduction to the post. Years later I would learn to love Fort Hood as eventually it became my home. But, for a bright eyed, bushy-tailed young man, the two weeks in the summer felt more like Boy Scout camp than a military exercise. As the Guardsmen met up at the National Guard motor pool, situated on North Fort Hood, just south of Gatesville, Texas, they seemed more interested in the fishing holes near our bivouac site than taking stock of the vehicles we were to take possession of and utilize for the next couple of weeks.

This was my first real introduction to the M88 recovery vehicle, which is legendary for its ability to tow an incredible amount of weight. I have personally seen a variant of the M88 pulling two fifteen-ton vehicles while pushing a third sixty-ton vehicle up a hill. Incredible from a maintenance stand point. Just about everything on the M88 weighs more than a person, which lends to caution; everything on that vehicle will either crush you, smash you, or squish you if you're not careful.

We rolled our vehicle out to the bivouac site and set up camp. Over the course of the next couple of weeks we did more sitting around waiting for something to happen than we did actually training. I remember sitting in my tent and sweating my tail off more than anything else. One little bit of training we did was qualification on our weapon systems. I qualified on the M2, .50 caliber machine gun (often referred to as the "Ma Deuce") and the M3A1, which was a .45 caliber machine gun often issued to armored vehicle crew members as a defensive weapon. The M2 is a superb weapon system. It hasn't changed much since it was first introduced just prior to World War I as an air defense weapon. The bullets it fires are large and rather ominous. I would hate for someone to fire this thing at me.

The M3 wasn't all that accurate, but it sure put lead down range fast. If you don't know what this weapon looks like just watch some old World War II movies like *The Dirty Dozen*. It's the gun used by Lee Marvin to shoot out some ropes. I don't think that is possible, given how hard it is to control .45 caliber rounds flying out what is essentially a tube with a firing pin and a barrel jutting out the front. It is the most simple of weapons, but truly a waste of ammo to fire it.

Anyway, we worked on a few vehicles from time to time but the bulk of our time was used playing football and drinking beer. I was apprehensive about drinking the beer until Dutch, still my NCOIC, pointed out that he would take the heat if I wanted to drink one or two. After all, like he said, if I was old enough to defend my country I should be old enough to drink a beer every now and then.

One afternoon we had just finished playing a rather vigorous game and were enjoying some beer when this colonel walks up to the group. Apparently, he was having issues with his vehicle and needed some help. Having been an officer's son, I was a little nervous so I hid my beer behind the box I was sitting on.

"I see you fellas have been playing football."

"Yes, sir!" was the general answer.

"Those beers look awful cold."

"You want one?" Dutch asked.

"No, I just need some help with my jeep. It seems to be pulling to the left a lot and it makes a loud clicking noise from time to time. Which one of you is the NCOIC?"

A huge grin crossed Dutch's face as he replied, "I'm the NCO—U—see!"

With that the entire group erupted with laughter. I'm not sure the colonel got the joke right away but after a few minutes he joined in the laughter. Of course afterwards we worked on his jeep and had it back on the road in a jiff. I just remember those times as being a bunch of friends hanging out together without many cares in the world. As always, times and situations change. I have lost contact with all of the fellas; only seeing a couple of them years later in a restaurant. It would be nice to see them all again, but I fear most have passed away by now.

IN PROCESSING AT FORT JACKSON, SOUTH CAROLINA

A FEW MONTHS PASSED AND SOMEWHERE IN THE MIX I GOT MARRIED TO the most beautiful gal from my home town. Now, I know some of ya'll might want to debate that fact but, it's my book so I win. She is the most beautiful and that's final. Besides, it's already written. If you want to pay tribute to your significant other—write your own book. At any rate, I was married and as married couples often do, we were soon expecting our first. Like a lot of young men at about nineteen, I had lots of dreams and motivation. What I lacked was experience and know-how. When my new bride told me the news I was conflicted, at best. I was happy about the prospect of being a father, but the timing stunk. She and I were both in our freshmen years in college and with her being pregnant; some hard decisions would have to be made.

At first I thought I could manage working and going to school at the same time. I had the huge expense of a pregnancy looming over my head. If I remember correctly, it was going to cost us about $10,000 for the birth. Since I didn't come from an independently wealthy family, I would have to find some way to pay this bill. As the due date approached, it became alarmingly clear to me that juggling two full-time, minimum wage jobs and trying to go to school was not going to work. All I was doing was working, driving, going to school and sleeping between my work breaks. It was when I fell asleep at the wheel one afternoon and ran off the road that I decided this course of action wasn't going to work out.

Ultimately, I had a heart to heart with my wife. I chose to upgrade my enlistment and join the active duty army. After the Gulf War, there was a huge calling for active duty soldiers. Since I was already a school trained mechanic, and it seemed the army is always short of mechanics, I was welcomed onto active duty with open arms. Only problem was with this huge influx of soldiers, there was a six month waiting list for in-processing for active duty. I was in a race with the baby's due date to get my butt activated so the army would pay for my child's birth. I made it with about a week to spare.

I remember it like yesterday. I boarded the plane on the 1st of the month for Fort Jackson, South Carolina. Upon arrival (there was about one hundred of us), we were herded to a barracks where we more or less sat and waited for all the paperwork to catch up. Every morning we rolled out for physical training and from time to time we were utilized as manpower for post cleanup detail. I really didn't mind the manual labor, because at least I knew I was going to receive a paycheck and the child's birth would be covered under insurance. I was content.

One morning about 0430, we were just rolling out of bed and beginning to get dressed when one of the NCOs hollered down the center of the open bay barracks, "JONES! JONES! Your kid was born this morning! Get your ass down to the CQ desk ASAP!"

A roar erupted from everyone in the barracks. I flung myself out of my bed and somehow I was fully dressed in my BDU uniform when I hit the ground (we normally slept in our PT uniform). I quickly pulled on my boots and ran down the center of the barracks, receiving well wishes and pats on my back along the way. By the time I was at the end of the floor I had somehow managed to tie my boots so I wouldn't trip over them while running down the stairs.

I reported to the CQ desk and was given a little piece of paper with a phone number to call. I spent the next two hours on the phone with my family. It was one of the most memorable moments of my life. I had a little girl to call my own. I was sitting on top of the world at this point.

One thing that confused me, though. After I hung up the phone I was placed on forty-eight hour watch. What that means is I had to sit in the CQ's office for the next forty-eight hours under constant observation. I was told this was for my own good as they didn't want me to go AWOL. Hell, I didn't want to go AWOL; I had joined the army for my family. I didn't want to dishonor them by going AWOL. This was the first of many times over the rest of my career where I would be made to put up with a bullshit situation because of someone else's behavior. Unfortunately, that is just the way weak leaders deal with a situation. Instead of treating folks in a manner befitting their actions, it is just assumed that if one person is capable of erratic behavior, then everyone else will behave erratically as well.

WILDFLECKEN

FROM FORT JACKSON I WAS SENT TO GERMANY FOR MY FIRST ACTIVE DUTY assignment. I had been to Germany before. I mean, after all, I was an army brat. Actually, I was born in Germany, at the military hospital in Landstul, Germany, in 1971. My father was reassigned there again in 1976. So, to say I was familiar with Germany would probably be a stretch of the truth as I had been so young. However, I had been there before.

I was assigned to a military intelligence battalion as a mechanic. I really didn't know what I would be doing there but I was sure they had vehicles that would need repair. The battalion was located near Wildflecken, Germany, (all the soldiers called it "Wild Chicken") and when I arrived, one of the first things I noticed was that everyone seemed to like to drink alcohol. I was still 19 years old and the drinking age in the states was 21 (yes, even back then…). However, the drinking age in Germany is 16 for beer and 18 for all other types of alcohol. So, being a fella who likes to drink I was in hog heaven!

To make things even better, there was a monastery on the hill outside of the post where the monks specialize in making beer. As the monks have been perfecting their process for close to six hundred years, their beer is just about perfect. Although I can't prove it, I've been told the beer they produce was number two on *Playboy's* list of the best beers in the world sometime in the early 1990s.

The first weekend I was in-country I was introduced to one of the local traditions. You see, in order for a soldier to be considered part of the "in" crowd, he had to walk up to this monastery, consume five liters of beer (a little more than a gallon) during the course of a night, then be able to walk home. The inductee didn't have to necessarily remember doing it; he just had to be able to do it. Well, when I first arrived, I wanted to be a cool kid, so I proceeded with the task. Needless to say, I don't remember much of what occurred after the first beer, nor do I remember the walk back to the barracks, but I did join the Five Liter Club. Based on how dirty my clothes were the morning after, I think I must have rolled down the hill.

The barracks parties back in those days are legendary. The amount of booze consumed probably would have killed a herd of horses. One thing I'll never understand is why soldiers who were stationed in Germany, the land of beer, would walk to the Post Exchange (the PX or general-purpose store) and buy cases of American beer only to cart them back to the barracks to drink. This never made sense to me. That would be like visiting France and eating at a McDonalds. I mean, why the hell make the trip if you're not going to indulge in the local cuisine. Just plain foolish it you ask me. Like in that Monty Python skit, "American beer is like making love in a canoe…It's fucking close to water."

DEXHEIM

I'D BEEN AT THE BATTALION FOR LESS THAN THREE MONTHS WHEN THE decision to close Wildflecken was made. The battalion was uprooted and moved to another post in Germany called Dexheim. Wildflecken was a large post as far as posts in Germany went, and Dexheim was a small one. A soldier had to run around Dexheim twice just to break a sweat. A funny thing about Dexheim is that there weren't many trees in the area. It must have been hundreds of years earlier when the Germans in the area chopped down all the trees (if there ever were trees there). The area surrounding the post was now mostly occupied by vineyards. There also was a town near Dexheim called Oppenheim. If you're a consumer of fine German wines, you must know of Oppenheimer wine. Well, the vineyards around Dexheim are where they grow their grapes. A fun thing to do was head out to the vineyards to do PT and snatch some of the grapes off the vines for breakfast. They were pretty tasty.

As a new, married soldier to the unit in Germany, the policy at the time was for a soldier to earn "command sponsorship" of his family. What this meant to me was, I had to spend some time in the billets while my new family was still in Texas living with my mother and father. I think the intent behind this policy was for me to prove I could get myself to work in the mornings and show that I was a good soldier before the army incurred the expense of moving my family to Germany. Before my family arrived, I had to secure an international driver's license, a car (1979 BMW 520i—wahoo!), and an apartment on post, about a 15 minute walk from work. Because of the unit move from Wildflecken to Dexheim, the whole process took about six months to accomplish. I was ecstatic about picking my wife and new daughter up from the airport and bringing them to their new home in Germany.

While living in the billets, one thing to note was the lack of operational toilets and showers. Dexheim had apparently originally been scheduled for closure, so the outgoing unit hadn't spent any time or money repairing the billets. I think on our floor there was only one or two that worked. The rooms appeared to be set up as one or two person rooms but because of the lack of operational facilities, the unit was forced to put as many as four people per room. Initially things were pretty tight. Eventually, over time, the barracks manager was able to get the facilities working correctly, which freed up billet space so those living in the barracks could spread out. I think eventually the more senior guys were in rooms by themselves and it was the junior ones with roommates.

In the room I occupied, there were two other guys. Our toilet didn't always flush, but if one were to keep a bucket of water next to the toilet, after you finished your business you could dump the bucket of water into the toilet and it would flush. We made do with our situation. For the most part, the guys I lived with were rather clean and both seemed to be decent fellas. One was from the east coast, the other the northwest coast, and I was from Texas, so we pretty much had all our bases covered. Two of us, the guy from the west coast and me, were new to the army and both of us were married. I was the only one with an expecting wife. The other guy was on his third assignment so he was a wealth of knowledge about army living. If I remember correctly he had plans to marry a gal from his home town but I don't remember if that ever happened or not.

This was a time before the huge influx of computers and home video games. Although they existed, those type of entertainment systems hadn't quite made it main stream. There were such things as large TVs, but they sure weren't flat screens and generally took up a lot of space. Besides, the only TV channel available to us was AFN (Armed Forced Network) which didn't have great programming. There was satellite TV, but for most soldiers it was cost prohibitive, so we found other ways of entertaining ourselves.

One way was to play card games, like Spades or Hearts. In my family, growing up, well, we loved to play games but neither Spades nor Hearts ever made the list. But, I enjoyed learning how to play. As a side note, while in the field, whenever there was a significant amount of downtime, the cards always came out and Spades or Hearts were the games of choice. Other activities included barracks barbeques and, of course, the aforementioned drunk feasts. Although I didn't partake, some of the gals were a little loose with their morals and would go with just about anybody who wanted a piece. A new experience for me.

THE NASTY NEIGHBOR

AS NOTED EARLIER, I EVENTUALLY WAS REUNITED WITH MY FAMILY. AFTER moving into our new home we settled into a viable routine. One afternoon I heard knocking at my door. It was one of my former roommates, the one from the west coast. He had secured an apartment in the same building as mine which, at first, I thought was a wonderful thing. He was such a nice guy. His wife, on the other hand, turned out to be something of a disaster.

After my wife and I received our household goods, we worked tirelessly to empty all the boxes and get rid of all the excess trash associated with moving. Something of note about Germany is, it is probably the best place in the world for a new couple in the army to start out. There (I don't know if it still the same) you could actually sign for furniture. As my wife and I were newlyweds from meager means, we didn't have all that much in the way of furniture. I think the largest piece we had was a rocking chair my father gave me. We didn't even have a baby's crib. One of my NCOs had ordered one from the PX and they had delivered two so he gave me one.

Once you first move into the apartment, there was a form to fill out and you annotated the type of furniture already in the apartment. At the bottom of the form you could select the type of furniture you wanted and in a day or two someone would deliver it to you. The only real problem was, no one was coordinating the different pieces of furniture, so you ended up with all sorts of color codes and motifs. But I guess beggars can't be choosers. At least we had furniture.

My new neighbor? I think they lived out of their boxes for the first year or so after they moved in. I'm not certain if they ever completely unpacked. Their apartment became so nasty we eventually quit visiting. It wasn't just the boxes, it was just everything. Trash piled up next to the door, down the hallway, and into the individual bedrooms. Trash—in bags mind you—just was never taken out. It wasn't like they had to go very far to throw the trash away. The dumpster was right outside their half of the stairwell. In reality, all they would have to do was open a window and toss the trash right into the dumpster…it was that close.

At first I thought it was a blessing to have a friend live so close. As my wife wanted to work and we needed a babysitter, I thought utilizing this asset might work out mutually—at first anyways. One Saturday afternoon there was an emergency looming. My wife was working and I had to go someplace I couldn't take my daughter, so I called on my new neighbor to watch my daughter. When I dropped her off I had just put a nice clean white "onesy" on her. My daughter hadn't started crawling just yet and spent hours pulling herself across the floor on her belly. When I returned an hour or so later that white onesy wasn't white anymore. I immediately threw that piece of clothing in the hamper and tossed the kid into the tub. Thoughts of all the nasty things she could have been crawling through made my stomach turn. I never again took my daughter over there.

Another friend of ours, a gal my wife worked with, lived on the same side of the stairwells this nasty neighbor did. One day my wife's co-worker was walking to her apartment, above the nasty one, when she smelled something just awful oozing from one of the apartments. At first she thought a rat had died inside the walls. She planned on calling the building manager after she located the source of the smell. Her nose led her to the door of the nasty one. The co-worker knocked on the door and when the nasty one opened the door an overpowering stench of death just about knocked the co-worker down.

Not wanting to offend the nasty one, the co-worker asked if everything was alright, fearing someone had died inside the apartment. The nasty one said everyone was happy and healthy (a real wonder considering how vile the apartment was). The co-worker noticed a hamster cage just inside the door and as she had an affinity for cute fuzz things said, "Oh, when did you get a hamster?"

The nasty one said, "About three weeks ago, it's been dead for a couple of days though." The source of the smell was discovered.

Did it end there? I don't think so. Eventually the nasty one got pregnant. My wife thought she would develop the "nesting" instinct and begin cleaning her house. For those women libbers out there: she didn't work, her husband did. I think if one member of the union works and the other doesn't, then the one that doesn't should clean the freaking house. Just the way I was raised. I'm not saying the working member has much of an excuse for living in squalor either. One of them should have cleaned it! I'm just of the mindset that the non-working spouse has more free time—especially if there are no kids in the mix. I digress...

About the time the nasty one was due to deliver, her husband's mother flew over for a visit. I remember the mother taking about a week or so and scrubbed that house clean as a whistle. The baby was born and all seemed to be shaping up...not for long though. I think almost immediately after the mother left the trash stopped finding its way to the dumpster. Now, with the addition of dirty diapers in the mix, a new aroma was added to the trash pile they called a home.

Maybe one of us should have called Child Protection Services about the situation. I really don't know. Those are really hard things to do in that kind of situation. It's not just a health hazard for the one household—It's a hazard to the whole building. But, on the other hand, he was a friend of mine...maybe that's why I should have called. Not something I am really proud of...but it did happen.

THE BIRDS

ONE THING TO NOTE ABOUT DEXHEIM WAS THE BIRDS. ON THE POST WERE a whole bunch of trees that probably had been planted by some well-meaning American commander in the past. German winemakers had chopped down all the trees in order to ward off birds. You don't have to be a rocket scientist to figure out that birds like to eat grapes and roost in trees. In the fall the soldiers of Dexheim were plagued with birds—several tens of thousands of them. The birds roosted in the trees, then at first light flocked to the vineyards to feast on the grapes. In the evening they'd flock back to the trees to roost again. You learned quickly not to park a car under a tree at Dexheim. The birds, after feasting all day on grapes, would paint a car in a couple of hours.

One Friday night a fellow soldier had left a BMW outside the bar on post because he was too drunk to drive. Why he drove to a bar that was about three hundred feet from the barracks is still a mystery. The soldier left it there for the weekend, and when he went to collect it Monday afternoon, the car was completely covered with bird droppings. He was rather dismayed and left it there for a couple of weeks. Everyone told him he needed to get his car washed before the droppings caused too much damage to the paint. When he finally decided to get his car and clean up the mess, the vehicle was a total loss. The acidity of the bird droppings actually had eaten through the body.

A little later the post commander decided to do something about our bird infestation. He had the soldiers conduct "bird patrol." This may have been the dumbest thing I've been a party to in my military career. We'd walk around the post and shoot "artillery simulators" into the trees to scare off the birds. The only problem was the birds had nowhere else to go, so they'd just fly around for a bit then land back in the trees. These bird patrols didn't do anything about the problem.

One girl I worked with was a bleeding-heart-liberal, bird-loving fruitcake. She claimed she shouldn't be forced to participate in the bird patrols, as she thought we shouldn't disturb the birds since they were there first. In her mind we were the invaders, not the birds. The commander bought off on this bullshit, and she was removed from the bird-patrol duty roster.

My wife worked at the local PX, where there were pictures of the post from back in the 1950s. It had been a German army post since before World War II. There was also an old German guy working at the PX who was born in the area and had lived there all his life. I saw a picture of the post when it had no trees and asked him where all the trees had come from. That's when I got the history of the post, the vineyards, and why there were no other trees in the area.

I took the picture to my commander and showed it to him. "I think this is proof that we were here before the birds," I said. The girl never liked me much after that, as she immediately was put back on the bird-patrol roster.

PICK YOUR OWN ROOMMATE!

ONE OF THE SILLIEST THINGS I HAVE EVER BEEN A PART OF WAS THE PRE-cursor program behind what was to become the BOSS program (Better Opportunity for Single Soldiers)—a program designed around trying to keep single soldiers from being abused and giving them opportunities to get out and experience the local area (be it Germany, Italy, Texas, or wherever the soldier finds him/herself). You see, prior to this program it was considered kosher to ask certain things of single soldiers that wouldn't be asked of married ones. For example, if there was a long tasking requiring one soldier and another shorter tasking requiring one soldier, back in the day, it wasn't considered an issue to send the single guy away for the long one and a married guy to the shorter one. Truth is, it shouldn't matter whether or not a soldier is married or not, they all should be treated equally.

Although on the surface this seems like it makes sense, the truth is… this decision is actually abusing a single soldier. A single soldier's free time is just as valuable as a married soldier's free time. Another type of abuse was, the 1SG grabbing a guy from the barracks to mow the grass in front of the company area. The grass in front of the company area is a common area and being a single soldier shouldn't make you more susceptible to additional duties. To mow the grass around the barracks is a different story. Additionally, back in the day, the NCOs used to inspect the single soldiers room on a daily basis, ensuring cleanliness. Married soldiers never had their quarters checked so once again there was a double standard. BOSS has fought to change all that. But before it was BOSS, it started off as something else.

At any rate, during this period in the army, the above concepts were just starting to form. The first I heard of this BOSS program it wasn't called BOSS. It was called SSQL[4]. One of the test runs for the SSQL program was, soldiers could pick their own roommates. This, on the

---

4. Single Soldier Quality of Life—if you ask me BOSS sounds better

surface, may sound like a good idea; however, not when you apply this to coed units like, say, an MI battalion?

In my company there were thirteen unwed female soldiers living in the barracks. As a result of this "pick your own roommate" policy these females were able to shack up with their boyfriends. Now, I'm not some old fogy who thinks sex out of wedlock is a big deal; after all I was unwed once. It became a huge problem when twelve of the thirteen females turned up pregnant. Now the commander has a deployment issue. Why, you might ask? To answer that question, it's because the army doesn't make it a policy to deploy pregnant females to a war zone, that's why.

To make matters worse, the first female to end up pregnant was one of limited morals. She, as was authorized, signed for a house on post in preparation of her looming family and started running a bed and breakfast out of it. She would offer dinner, some entertainment, and then breakfast, if the price was right. That's right; she was running a brothel out of her house. Some of the other pregnant females saw this as a way to gain some quick cash and started following her lead. The first female saw herself as the "Madam" and wanted part of the other girls' action because it was her idea. This is where things began to unravel. Next thing you know they are fighting amongst each other and the word gets out to the wrong ears and WHAMO! An investigation is started. All of this in the name of single soldier equality. Some people take things a bit too far.

One of the females from my section was talking about doing that exact thing. I told her, even though I wasn't an NCO yet, I didn't approve. Her ultimate plan was to have thirteen kids while in the army. She figured, if she could space them out just right, thirteen was enough to where she would never have to go to the field, take an APFT—or do PT at all for that matter (this was a time before all the "pregnant" PT hype). The army would have to promote her eventually, by her thinking, without her having really to do anything. I was appalled by this lack of moral turpitude. I asked her what she planned on doing with all those kids? Her answer? To send them back to her mother to raise. Wow, a complete lack of responsibility. I was completely flabbergasted that anyone could even conceptualize something like that. This was my first introduction to the army as a "welfare" program. I don't know if she ever proceeded with her plan. Or, if the army promoted her like she thought it would have to. I do know she had two kids by two different fathers before I moved away. Shameless.

NATO ADAPTER

I KNOW YOU'VE HEARD ABOUT THINGS BEING FOOL PROOF. YOU KNOW, things that even fools can't mess up or break? Well, there isn't anything made that's soldier proof. If there is a way to break it, a soldier somewhere has found a way to do it. Believe you me, that is the solid truth! Case in point, while working as a tracked vehicle mechanic in Germany, I had the honor of replacing the entire wiring system on one of are armored personal carriers. Here is how I found myself with that dubious honor.

From time to time, as you probably already know, the batteries on a vehicle die for one reason or another, so it has to be jumped off by another vehicle. As most vehicles in the army are diesel engines and diesels require more cranking amps to turn the engine over, the vehicles require more batteries to provide the power. Generally speaking, the larger the vehicle, the larger the engine, and more batteries required. The vehicle I was working on in this story required four batteries, as an example.

Since most folks out there don't have a shred of mechanical ability, the army came up with a system to jump vehicles off that is supposed to be fool proof. It's called a "slave cable." The batteries are wired to a cylinder shaped device where the inside is the positive and the outside is the negative, with a rather stout insulator in between the two. The cable simply slips over the cylinder and presto, you have the perfect connection. That is, of course, until you add in our NATO (North Atlantic Treaty Organization) partners.

For some reason, NATO went with a different set-up. Theirs is a similar cylinder shaped device but instead of going with the inside/outside format, they went with pins that were offset from the center for their positive and negative connectors. Their system isn't incompatible with ours. To solve this dilemma, the army came up with "NATO Adaptors," which are a smallish device that fits over our version of the slave system and adapts it to theirs. Like I said, the pins are offset, so this combination should still be more or less fool proof.

Now, for a reason I can't explain, the army decided to make some of its vehicle US standard and other vehicles NATO standard when it came to this slave system. Well, there was this young soldier who needed a jump for her vehicle and pulled a HMMWV around to supply the charge. The tracked vehicle was NATO standard and the HMMWV was US standard so she decided to use an adaptor and drive on with her mission. Problem was, she couldn't get the NATO adaptor to fit into her tracked vehicle's slave device. Her decision? Get a hammer.

She pounded on that thing until it fit nice and flush. Next, she grabbed the slave cable and proceeded to plug it in. It's a wonder she didn't electrocute herself. The arc was rather impressive. As soon as the connection was made, the entire wiring harness decided to melt. And, guess who the lucky mechanic was that had to fix it…me. Some people shouldn't be allowed to touch machinery.

BIRTH OF A GERMAN

MY WIFE AND I HAD BEEN IN GERMANY FOR ABOUT A YEAR OR SO WHEN she informed me she was once again with child. I was ecstatic. The first thing I did was trot down to the PX and buy a box of cigars—passing them out to everyone I saw. It's pretty much common knowledge that the two most enjoyable things about having kids is, first, making them and then, say twenty years later when they finally move out of the house. Everything else ranks somewhere in between. As a side note, one of my more enjoyable moments of my wife's pregnancy was tapping the brakes of the car while she was strapped in and having to go pee. Sadistic I know, but still funny.

I'll fast forward to the actual delivery. The night before my wife went into labor I just happened to have been on a 24 hour duty so I had the next day off. In today's army, there is a lot of consideration given to an expecting parent. I am talking about deploying a soldier late, leaving them behind, or placing them on light duty until the delivery of the child. Back in the day? Well, let's just say the standing policy was pretty much, "If the army had wanted you to have a family, they would have issued you one." After the birth we were allowed to have a couple of weeks leave, but it wasn't mandatory. I suppose it isn't today, but it's strongly encouraged. I've left guys behind before a deployment so they could bear witness to the birth of their child. As a brilliant lady put it to me, "You have to be there for the planting, but not the harvest!"

Anyways, I guess karma was on my side as I did have the day off. In fact, I had just come home from my duty when my wife informed me it was time to head to the hospital. Now, years earlier when I was born in Germany, I was born in a US hospital in Landstul, Germany. By the time of my second child's birth, almost all the US hospitals were closed and the majority of the pregnancy was monitored by Germans in German hospitals. The lay person might not think this is such a big deal, but I don't speak German. Although a lot of German doctors speak some

English, what about the nurses? Midwives? Hospital staff? There is no guarantee these folks speak English. So, therein lies the problem.

I rushed my wife to the hospital and into the ER. Although the staff member I was talking to didn't speak much English, all I really had to do was point to my wife's belly and make an explosion noise and the staff immediately understood. They put my wife into the "I'm in labor room," then the midwife grabbed my hand and hustled me out of the room. Truthfully, although I did have a daughter, if you remember, I wasn't there at her birth so this is all a new experience for me. I really didn't know what to expect. The midwife shuttled me down the hallway to a closet. She pulled a bed out of the closet and made a "push this" sign and I followed her back up the hallway, onto an elevator, and then we went two floors up. Out of the elevator and down the hallway to what was to be my wife's room. Why the Germans didn't keep the beds on the same floor of the rooms, I really can't explain. I didn't take the opportunity to ask either as a couple of more pressing things were on my mind. I spent the next half hour or so setting up the room, making the bed, and pulling the crib out of another closet. I felt like a janitor.

I had just finished the room when the midwife came rushing into the room. At first I thought I had done something wrong because she seemed rather stern. She led me into the delivery room and there on the birthing station sat my wife. She had an intern standing next to her who apparently spoke English. I was introduced and took my place next to my wife. I held her hand through the whole process.

I think we had been in the hospital for a total of forty-five minutes when my wife's contractions climaxed. I remember the intern saying, "Push!" and the midwife saying, "Nein! Nein! Kein Arzt!" (For those German-challenged, it means, "No! No! No Doctor!") About the time the midwife was holding the baby, the doctor came walking in the room, whistling, with his hands in his pocket. "Oh, everything seems to be just fine," and with that, he left the room. I mean, what the hell was he being paid for? The midwife did all the work. Maybe I'm in the wrong line of work! By the way, remember how I said I was holding my wife's hand? Well, she squeezed the hell out of it. I think she may have snapped a couple of bones in there somewhere. She isn't but about 120 pounds soaking wet (sans pregnancy) and I didn't expect her to be able to force my pinkie knuckle to meet my index finger knuckle. My hand really hurt! Now, for all you woman libists out there, I know pregnancy hurts. Although I had a hand in the pregnancy it still doesn't excuse the pain in my hand. So, any of you fella's out there with a pregnant wife—hold her hand at your own risk.

Anyway, my wife was really craving a sub-sandwich. I didn't know of any German sandwich shops in the area but there was one on a US post nearby. After my wife was moved into the room I made up for her, I beat feet to the sub shop and ordered her favorite sandwich. Problem was, I got lost on the way back. Somehow I got twisted around. What should have been about a thirty minute trip turned into a two hour trip. When I finally returned, my wife was concerned I had fallen victim to an accident of sorts. I put her mind to rest. I looked down upon my wife and my new son. I called him Raymond Lewis Jones, Jr. Every father deserves a junior.

THE STARTER

ANOTHER KNUCKLEHEAD I RAN INTO WAS AN NCO IN OUR SECTION WHO was somewhat of a know-it-all. He was new to the section and never had worked on the type of vehicles we had in our battalion, but since working on this type of vehicle was part of our job description, he tried to pretend he knew more than he really did. Those of us who had repaired these vehicles had worked out ingenious ways to replace certain parts that were difficult to reach and therefore difficult to work on.

One time we were replacing a starter, which weighed about forty-five pounds and was in a most inconvenient location—on the side of the engine right below the radiator. There were three bolts that held the starter on the engine block, and two of the three bolts were pretty easy to get to. The third, however, was almost impossible. We, the experienced, had devised a tool that made the difficult rather easy. It was a two-and-a-half-foot piece of rebar tapped to fit into the bolt hole, so all we had to do was screw in the rebar, slide the starter to where it was supposed to sit, then tighten the two easy bolts. Once everything was set in place, we'd remove the rebar and with a couple of half-inch extensions on the end of a ratchet, we'd place and tighten the third bolt. Easy enough.

This NCO, however, was going to show us "young'uns" a thing or two. A slight individual could fit under the radiator and reach that bitch bolt rather easily, but not the other two. The problem was that after the starter was in place, the individual under the starter/radiator wouldn't have enough room to climb out.

Well, the NCO climbed under the radiator and got the bitch bolt in place and held the starter in place while we tightened the other two bolts. It was almost lunchtime, and after we finished the job, we climbed off the track, cleaned up, and went to chow—leaving the NCO to his fate of being stuck under the radiator. As we were leaving the motor pool, we heard all sorts of screaming and cursing. We all smirked at one another as we moved right along to chow.

When we got back from the chow hall, the motor sergeant was waiting for us with a list of little "chores" we were to complete before the day was over, but that extra work was worth it, since that know-it-all NCO didn't stay in our section very long.

THE STOVE

WE HAD THIS OTHER KNUCKLEHEAD SERGEANT WHO WAS SOMEWHAT OF A prick. He had the innate ability to piss off everyone around him, merely with his presence. One particular time, on a Monday, I showed up to formation for physical training (PT, normally held at 0630 hours) and informed him that the stove in my house wasn't functioning and that I had called in a work order to get it fixed. A work order on an appliance such as a stove was an emergency work order and the Department of Public Works (DPW) told me to wait in the house, as I was the hand receipt holder, and they'd be by as soon as possible to fix it.

I told the sergeant about my troubles and said I'd have to miss motor stables[5]. His response was, "No way in hell are you going to miss motor stables." He told me to have my wife wait for the repairman, and I was to be in the motor pool at 0900 hours. I told him that wouldn't work for several reasons: first, the house was assigned to me, and DPW would only deal with me; second, I thought it was inappropriate for me to leave my spouse and two young children alone in a house with a stranger; third, my wife had to be at work at 1000. The NCO told me to shut up and do PT, and he'd figure out a solution to my problem. I went and did PT until about 0730, when this NCO found me and informed me that he had a solution.

His solution was to have another soldier sit in my house and wait for DPW. At first I thought he was joking, and I laughingly asked, "Who?" He replied, "Mac." Well, this kind of set me off. Not only was he serious about having this other soldier sit in my house, but also this other soldier was from my section and was of the same military operational specialty

---

5. Motor stables is a term which has been adapted to mean a specific time to perform maintenance on your vehicles. Generally this occurs on the first day of the work week. I think the term goes back to when the army had horses and the soldiers cared for their horses

(MOS or job description). It wasn't about someone missing motor stables; it was about *me* missing motor stables.

I told this NCO, in rather colorful language, that his idea wouldn't work. He locked me up (made me stand real still with my hands behind my back) and began to rip me a new one. Fortunately, around that time, passing by this scene was the battalion maintenance officer (BMO) and the battalion maintenance technician (BMT; a special breed of soldiers, they're technical experts and revered as gods among junior enlisted folks). They heard this NCO yelling at me, and I was sort of yelling back, so they naturally asked, "What's going on?" The NCO responded that I was disrespectful to him and needed some correctional training. The BMT looked at me and asked me what was going on. I explained in detail all that had transpired. The BMT told me to go home, clean up, and take care of my business. When I was done with DPW, I was to report directly back to him. He then looked at the NCO and said, "Follow me."

After DPW had repaired my stove, I reported to the BMT. He told me everything was all right, and I wouldn't be facing any kind of Uniform Code of Military Justice (UCMJ or punishment) for disrespecting the NCO. A couple of hours later, when that NCO tracked me down, he'd lost some of the perk in his step and some of the color in his face. He then told me that if I ever needed anything—anything at all—he was the man to see. He'd help me out in any way he could. I have no idea what the BMT told him, but that NCO was a bit of a better sergeant at that moment. Unfortunately it didn't last long.

THE HATCH

ANOTHER TIME, WHILE WE WERE IN THE FIELD, THIS NCO (THE SAME NCO from the previous story) put himself in charge of the tracked vehicle recovery team. I was the assigned operator for the recovery track and had a little bit of experience with it. I'd been school trained and assigned for about a year when this yahoo came on board. He decided he was the better recovery expert, since he was the sergeant. Just about anything I mentioned or suggested was automatically wrong. So while he was in charge, I just went around being wrong a whole bunch.

One time, while we were out in the field, the springing mechanism for the driver's hatch had begun to lose its springiness. I tied the hatch down when I was driving so I wouldn't get knocked in the head if I hit a bump and the hatch came loose from its perch. This NCO decided to reverse the springs in the hatch, so instead of the hatch popping open, it would slam shut. Now these hatches aren't light; they must weigh around forty or fifty pounds, and the additional pressure from the reversal of the springs must have added several times the usual amount of pressure.

The normal crew for one of these recovery tracked vehicles consisted of three members: the driver, the track commander (TC), and the rigger. Each position had an assigned seat on the vehicle, and because the NCO wanted to be the driver, I was sitting in the TC's seat, and one of my buddies was in the rigger's seat. We were towing an M113 back to the unit maintenance collection point (UMCP). It was night, and because we were training, we were driving in blackout drive (with no lights on). I remember it being a nice moonlit night, so we didn't have our night-vision goggles on. Suddenly the vehicle began to make little jerky movements. Then it swerved to the right, and finally it stopped abruptly. The rigger and I were looking at each other, not really sure what had happened, when over the intercom we heard a faint "Somebody help me."

The rigger then sprang into action. He leapt out of his seat and hightailed it toward the driver's hatch. There was no way I could match his speed or reaction time, so I did the next best thing; I turned on the lights. These recovery vehicles have flood lights all over them. Once one of these vehicles is lit, it becomes as bright as day in and around the vehicle. Only when I climbed my slow butt out of the hatch did I discover what had happened. We had hit a bump, and the hatch had come loose from its perch and smacked the NCO right in the head. He was staggering around like he was punch-drunk.

The rigger and I waited several minutes until the sergeant recovered some sense of orientation. Then he looked at me as if I'd done something to make the hatch pop loose. He asked for a wrench so he could "fix" the problem. After I fetched a wrench for him, he loosened several bolts and was convinced that what he had done would fix the problem. I looked at what he had done, and I didn't know how the bolts he had loosened would do anything except make the hatch release from its perch more easily. I made mention of this to him, and he flashed a look at me that quickly reminded me how wrong I was about everything. Still, in my wrong way, I suggested he use the strap to ensure the hatch would stay in the locked position. He told me to shut up and climb back up into my seat. What was I thinking?

We began to roll down the road and made it about four hundred meters when the vehicle did the exact same thing. It began to make little jerky movements. Then it swerved to the right and finally stopped abruptly. Pretty much the same set of events as the last time occurred as the rigger sprang into action and I turned on the lights. When I finally climbed down front, the hatch had worked its way loose and smacked that idiot in the head again. Finally the sergeant grabbed the strap I had suggested he use and strapped the hatch down. Afterward he seemed to think that the idea of strapping the hatch down had been his idea and that it was a rather bright one.

Two days later, while we were repairing the M113, we had some downtime while another set of mechanics replaced the engine. The NCO decided to make good use of our downtime and had me clean the recovery vehicle—from the inside out. After I opened several of the hatches and crawled inside the belly of the vehicle, I found some .50 caliber shells. I thought this was rather interesting, as I'd never fired live .50 caliber shells from the vehicle, and the vehicle had been in Desert Storm. The shells must have been remnants from the desert. I was pulling the shells out of the belly of the recovery vehicle when the NCO took an interest in what I was doing and worked himself really close to my backside. All I felt was something tickling the back of my neck, and I thought it was a fly, so I swung backward in an effort to swat it. Instead of swatting a fly, I ended up smacking the NCO in the nose (which I think was broken from the previous incident). I do believe he wanted to kill me. He wrote me up for "assaulting an NCO" and recommended I receive some form of non-judicial punishment. Fortunately the BMT got his hands on the paperwork and did a little investigating. When he discovered the true nature of the "assault," he made sure no action was taken against me and took care of the situation.

HOW TO SNAP
A WINCH CABLE

ONE DAY WHILE SUPPORTING THE BATTALION IN HOHENFELS, GERMANY, my crew was called out to recover a broke-down vehicle. Again, the crew on our vehicle consisted of three fellas. There was an NCO, a mechanic (me), and a rigger. The NCO was supposed to be in charge of the whole crew; the mechanic was there to maintain and troubleshoot vehicular issues; and the rigger was supposed to be a recovery specialist for pulling vehicles out of the mud or flipping them upright if the need arose. Our crew? Well, the NCO was the same fella from the earlier story (The Hatch) and the rigger was a generator mechanic—who was good at his trade—but didn't know a thing about recovery. I was probably the only one in that battalion who had actually gone through the army's recovery training program.

As mentioned earlier, the battalion I was supporting was a Military Intelligence (MI) battalion. They had all sorts of neat little toys to play with. One of these toys was called a MILKY system. I never knew what the acronym MILKY stood for, or if I did, I quickly chose to forget it because all I was really focused on was the maintenance of the MILKY's carrier. To tell the truth, MI folks were typically rather nerdy. Now don't get me wrong, they were (and are), for the most part, pretty nice guys and gals. They were just into a lot of high speed equipment I never really understood how it worked, and this stuff was more or less out of my realm of "wanting to understand." So, I let them be them and I was me. All of us were happy.

To kind of sum up the smarts of some of these characters, well, one day a guy gave me a copy of Stephen Hawkins, *A brief history of space and time.* Since then (more than twenty years have passed) I have tried to read and understand that book three times. I almost got through half of it once before I had to set it aside before my brain exploded. The guy who gave it to me? Well, he told me it was a "quick read." We use to call the MI guys "cone-heads", a reference to the Dan Aykroyd character from, *Saturday Night Live.* You know, too smart to tie their shoes. The kind of fella I'm talking about could define Pi to the hundredth decimal point but have a hard time understanding the whole "lefty lousy-righty tighty" concept when it comes to nuts and bolts. Yeah, you know the type I'm talking about.

Anyways, we were called out on this trouble call to recover this MILKY that had broken down for one reason or another. When we arrived, it was a bright sunny day and the temperature was probably in the mid 50's or so. It was winter time in Germany, and if any of you out there have been in the field in Germany, you know that if you don't like the weather all you have to do is wait a minute and it will change. I, and some of my fellow soldiers, have often wondered if the army has a weather machine of sorts and the senior brass can jack with us lowly peons by flipping a switch and changing the weather on a dime. I bring this up because just after we arrived on site for the trouble call, the weather decided to change from "nice and sunny" to "cold and shitty."

The vehicle was on the side of a hill at about a thirty percent grade (rather steep). We pulled up and started to troubleshoot the vehicle when all of a sudden the wind picked up and it started to snow. The temperature dropped probably twenty degrees in a matter of about thirty minutes or so. As it was late in the afternoon when we arrived, the decision was made that we would probably want to spend at least one night out there. So the rigger and I broke out the tent, along with the Yukon stove, and began to set up camp. After we got the tent set up we rejoined the NCO who was still working on the vehicle.

Over the next couple of hours the sun began to set and the weather continued to deteriorate. It got so cold out there we were having trouble hanging on to our tools so it was decided we should break for the night and regroup in the morning. Now, I am from Texas. The word "Blizzard" rarely comes up; however, I think that night was the first blizzard I had ever been a part of. If it wasn't a blizzard, then it's as close as I want to come to one. You fella's up north are probably thinking I'm a wimp. Well, when it comes to cold weather I'm a down right sissy. That's why I live in Texas, after all.

That night, sometime around midnight, I was pulling fire guard (fire guards guard against fire). We were in need of a fire guard because we had the Yukon stove on for warmth, I was getting sleepy so I decided I was going to smoke a cigarette to try and wake myself up. Since it was so cold outside and the other fella's were asleep I thought I would be slick and smoke while inside the tent (a big no no for those who don't know). I lit up and smoked away.

When I was finished, I began looking for a place to put the cigarette butt. I didn't want to open the tent door because the cold wind would wake my tent mates up and I didn't want to do that. I decided to throw the butt into the Yukon stove. My thinking was the flames on the inside would burn any evidence of my cigarette and I would be good to go.

The Yukon stoves work off gasoline. There is a little carburetor inside the box that regulates the amount of gas, a little vent that regulates the amount of oxygen, and when everything is working perfectly the stove keeps everything nice and cozy. These are all things I wish I knew before that night, because when I opened the vent in order to toss in my cigarette butt I had a flame shoot out of the front of that thing that burned my eyelashes, eye brows, and most of the three day shadow I was sporting around.

The flame had the secondary effect of scaring the hell out of my tent mates as they both jumped out of their beds yelling, "THE TENTS ON FIRE!!!"

There I sat on my cot with the remnants of the hair on my face smoking. By the way, to this day I don't know what happened to that cigarette butt.

We spent two days in our shelter before the wind quit howling and snow stopped falling. (I quit smoking in the tent by the way…). Thank god we had that tent. I'll hand it to the army and its shelters; they truly hold up to weather like that. It was nice and cozy inside our little hooch.

When the weather finally broke and the sun once again decided to make an appearance, we had to dig our way out of the shelter. We spent probably half that day just digging the vehicles out of the snow. It was rather apparent we weren't going anywhere for at least another day so we could let the snow melt. Once again we began to troubleshoot the broken vehicle. After a couple of hours it was determined we couldn't fix the vehicle on site and it would have to be hauled back to the maintenance collection point as the transmission was blown and we didn't carry spare transmissions around with us. Too heavy and bulky.

The next morning it was still rather cold outside and overnight the temperature had again reached the freezing point. There was a nice coat of ice over just about everything. As we were pulling everything together so we could tow the vehicle to the maintenance point, the battalion executive officer (XO) showed up in order to get an update as to the status of vehicle. The XO asked a simple question.

"We need this MILKY in the fight (simulation). Is there any way we can drag it up the hill?"

My NCO, being the knucklehead he was, said, "Hell ya! We can pull anything!"

Me, being the only recovery specialist in the group, well, I knew dragging that vehicle up that hill in these weather conditions was next to impossible to accomplish. It's a simple matter of weight versus traction. The recovery vehicle weighed just over thirty tons. The MILKY weighed just under. Although the recovery vehicle was rated to tow close to forty tons, the MILKY was sitting on the side of a hill. If it had been at the base of the hill and we had a running start to gain momentum, then it might have been possible. But, starting on that steep of a grade and covered with ice? No way in hell would we be able to drag the MILKY up the hill.

But, we tied onto the MILKY anyways and tried. Like I predicted, all that happened is the tracks spun wildly. The NCO was revving the engine so high I thought he would blow the engine in the recovery vehicle as well. He thought he could get more traction if he continued to spin the tracks in place, creating heat and friction against the ground. All he ended up doing was digging a couple of ruts and coating the front of MILKY with mud.

After that failed attempt, we unhooked the MILKY and he pulled the recovery vehicle out of the ruts and drove it up the hill about a hundred feet or so. Then he turned the vehicle around. I had no idea what he was doing so I just stood there and watched. After he had turned the vehicle completely around he began to drop the spade into the ground. That's when it became clear to me how much of an idiot he truly was. The spade is a flat steel brace that runs the width of the vehicle, designed to stabilize it during winching operations. He intended to winch the broken vehicle up the hill.

Now, I'm not sure what the exact equation is for figuring out the amount of mechanical advantage required to pull a thirty ton vehicle up a thirty percent slope covered with ice but I guess it would have to be at least thirty percent added to the weight of the towed vehicle. Makes sense to me. To the NCO? Nope. Not a bit of sense. I know this because I tried to explain to him why his plan wouldn't work. He just told me to, "Shut up and hook it up!"

You see, the main winch on the recovery vehicle was rated at thirty tons. What that means is, once paid out it will reel in up to thirty tons. You can almost double that capacity by adding a snatch block to the operation. If you were to attach the snatch block to the stuck vehicle, run the cable over the pulley, then attach the cable to the recovery vehicle then you have almost doubled the winching capacity (30 tons x 2 – (10%) = 54 tons). This can be repeated as many times as required or until you run out of snatch blocks or cable.

I think the above concept was a bit too much for the NCO. I tried to explain that he needed to move closer to the MILKY so we could add a snatch block to the operation but that didn't fly. Next, I tried to explain to him that you don't want to pay out the entire cable as it might snap. If he had just moved twenty-five feet closer to the MIKLY we would have been able to add a snatch block…if only.

We ran out the cable, hooked it up to the MIKLY, then everybody stood back because if (when) this cable snapped it would have enough force to cut a man in half. If you haven't guessed yet, the cable snapped. And, just so you know, when a cable snaps it makes a strange eerie whipping sound. Almost like a high pitched moan. Something I don't want to experience again.

Some of you might ask, what happened to the MILKY? Well, it never even budged. Ultimately we had to hook up to it and drag it back to the maintenance collection point where we spent another cold night replacing the transmission. Lots of fun.

THE NEW MAILROOM CLERK

I GUESS THE BMT HAD HAD ENOUGH OF THIS NCO'S (AGAIN THE SAME GUY from the previous stories) shenanigans because when a special duty assignment came up for the post mailroom he volunteered this NCO for the job. Normally a cushy job like post mailroom clerk would go to a guy or gal who was deserving. In this case, however, I am sure they picked a fella who they just wanted out of their hair for a little while. Whatever the reason, this NCO found himself in mailroom clerk school and ultimately sitting in the mailroom doing mailroom clerk type things for the next eight months or so.

During this time period I had decided I was finally an adult and I thought I would announce my adulthood to the world by ordering a subscription to *Playboy* magazine. One would think having a wife and a couple of kids would be enough of an announcement but when I was an adolescent I had always wanted a subscription so now that I was out on my own I decided to go for it.

I received maybe four copies of my magazine and then they stopped coming for some reason. You have to understand this was in the early 1990's, although email existed in a limited form, those of us who were average Joes had never heard about it. We did everything via snail mail. I did have a phone in my house capable of calling the States and Playboy did have a "toll free" phone number but, it wasn't toll free from Germany. So I wrote Playboy a letter complaining about missing an issue and waited for their response.

A couple of weeks later I received a letter back from them apologizing about the missing magazine and they claimed to have sent another copy. I never received it. Additionally, I didn't receive any subsequent issues either. After a couple of months dancing around with this issue, I finally decided to just cancel the subscription and get on with my life.

Unbeknownst to me at the time, several other folks weren't receiving their mail either. Everything culminated when one afternoon a spouse approached the NCO mailroom clerk and asked about a magazine she had ordered for her husband. Now, I don't know all the details because I wasn't there at the time. However, after talking with several folks I pieced together these little tidbits of information. Apparently, her husband was a real outdoorsman type of guy and she had ordered him a *Field and Stream* type of magazine for his birthday. I am guessing they had some type of gimmick along with the subscription because she was looking for a gift along with the magazine.

Because mail did take a little while to get to us, she had ordered the magazine a month or two prior to his birthday. Her plan was to collect all the magazines and the gift and wrap them up as a present. The magazines never came. For weeks she would walk into the mailroom anticipating her items to be there, only to be disappointed. A couple of times she would walk over to the mailroom clerk's office and ask him if he had just misplaced her stuff and he would always answer that he hadn't seen it.

One afternoon after the mailroom clerk told her he hadn't seen her magazine, she happened to look down and saw a magazine on the mailroom clerk's desk, open, and it appeared to be a field and stream type magazine so she flipped it to the cover and lo and behold, it was addressed to her husband. She immediately called the authorities and complained to them about this mailroom clerk reading her husband's magazine.

The resulting investigation discovered that this wasn't a onetime incident. Apparently, this mailroom clerk had been taking people's mail for months. When they investigated his house they found magazines, boxes, and all sorts of mail paraphernalia all over his house. No doubt my *Playboy* magazines were amongst the list of mail stolen. Now, I truly don't know what happened to this guy as the army doesn't announce the results of its judicial findings in a popular media outlet. However, I am sure the guy is still sitting in Manheim Prison taking a daily ass pounding for all his stupidity and troubles. Some folks get what they deserve.

SUPPORTING REFORGER

THE REFORGER (**REinFORce GERmany**) EXERCISE I WENT ON WAS AN exercise that was a remnant of the cold war. The idea, for those interested, was for the forces in Europe to act as a buffer and absorb the initial onslaught of the Soviet horde while the rest of the army would eventually land in Europe to save the day. This was the whole plan in a nutshell. By the time I was in Germany, the wall had fallen, the Soviets weren't a threat anymore because they didn't exist, and the only real threat was the collapse of those former soviet bloc countries. But, we still did RE-FORGER—just in case, I suppose.

My part in this REFORGER was to act as a recovery specialist in the event a vehicle broke down or wrecked and it needed to be recovered. During the two week exercise (or at least the two weeks I was part of this exercise) we only had one vehicle break down that we couldn't fix on the spot.

I need to make a break in the story so I can explain the situation for those not used to the 1990's and the American-German political relationship. The German government loved our money, both the US government's money and our personal paychecks as we spent a lot of money in their economy. If a cow was killed because of our training efforts the US government would pay for that cow, all the lost revenue associated from milk sales of that cow, plus all of the offspring it would never have now that the cow is dead for (I think) three generations. Kind of a crock of shit if you ask me, however, that is the way that it was. But, the Germans didn't like us running around their countryside tearing up their land. We would pay huge amounts of money associated with damage to the landscape–especially with contaminated waste like oil, anti-freeze, or fuel spillage.

I'm not one to harbor the illegal spillage of contaminated wastes but some of their issues were just plain crazy. If we were to accidently spill some oil while working on a vehicle, then a hole would have to be dug that extended twelve inches surrounding the spillage. Everything would have to be placed in special bags and then the hole would have to be filled in with clean dirt. A little ridiculous if you ask me. There is a difference between a little spill and the Exxon-Valdez incident.

So, back to the story, we dragged that vehicle back to a German motor pool and proceeded with pulling the pack so the repairs could be made. It took us a little more than a day to troubleshoot the problem, find a suitable repair part, then return the vehicle to an operational condition. We weren't breaking any records but we were working as fast as we could, given the circumstances. In the process, some of the anti-freeze had leaked out and was running down the storm drain located at the end of the motor bay. The Germans didn't seem to care about the antifreeze as I'll bet their motor pools were built like ours and had a contaminated waste separator built into the storm drain.

The vehicle we were working on was in high demand for the current operation and the NCO of our section was giving regular updates to our higher headquarters. Apparently we weren't working fast enough because the Assistant Division Commander in charge of support (ADC-S, a one star general) paid us a visit just to check on our disposition. He flew in on his helicopter and landed on the German's parade field and the exhaust from the turbine engines on the helicopter had burned two perfect circles on the nice green grass of the parade field.

The ADC-S was walking with a herd of German fella's and I recognized one of them to be the German post commander as his picture was hanging everywhere on the post. The general, after watching us and noticing the antifreeze leak, proceeded to chew my NCOs butt for not being more careful. He went back to the German post commander and apologized for the mess. The German commander seemed less worried about our antifreeze leak and more upset about the two holes burnt in his parade field. I don't think the one star ever really understood why the German commander was upset. Some people just can't take a hint nor see their own mistakes, but are quick to point to others.

THE CUC-V

WE HAD ANOTHER CHARACTER IN THIS UNIT WHO WAS RATHER UNIQUE and whom I also classify as a knucklehead. I believe he's the only person to have arrived at his first unit as a private second grade (PV2) then reach his end term of service (ETS, the day a soldier separates from the army and becomes a civilian) from the same unit without ever having been promoted to private first class (PFC). This soldier would either fail his PT test or the height-weight screening—never at the same time, but one or the other at any given time.

One time he was driving a civilian utility combat vehicle[6] at Hohenfels, a training area in Germany, while smoking a cigarette, which wasn't authorized. He then dropped the cigarette onto the floorboard. At this point he instinctively dove after the cigarette and inadvertently ran the vehicle off the road. The CUC-V was a total loss, but surprisingly he wasn't injured. The aftereffect of the accident was a Report of Survey[7] that held him liable for the loss to the government at an amount that exceeded $9,000, payable out of his paycheck at a half month's pay for the rest of the time he was on active duty.

Another time this stellar soldier had the opportunity to shine his stuff was when he ETS'ed from the army. To describe this soldier a little bit, one would have to look no further than his teeth. He had the most crooked teeth I've ever seen. I mean, he must have had either the most technically advanced toothbrush or the most dexterous fingers in order to keep them brushed. About a year or so before his ETS date, he began a series of dental surgeries and other dental work in an effort to straighten his teeth. After many hours of frustration and confusion on the part of the dentist and hours of pain for the soldier, the dentist decided to pull

---

6. A Chevy Blazer, also known as a "CUC-V"
7. An investigation that assesses financial liability

all of the soldier's teeth and put in dentures. This soldier now had a fresh set of shiny new dentures.

Several months later, he finally ETS'ed from the army, and I happened to be the Staff-Duty driver—the guy who drives the Staff-duty officer around or just makes runs to the PX or the shoppette for munchies. One of the services we provided was the one-way delivery of ETS'ing soldiers from the army to the airport. I took this soldier to the airport one early Saturday morning. Because he was more or less a friend of mine, I decided to wait with him for his plane. At some point I noticed he didn't have his teeth in and asked him what he had done with them. He frantically searched through his bags for his dentures but to no avail. Then he slipped me a twenty and asked me to mail him his teeth, as he probably had left them on the nightstand next to his bed. I agreed, and as soon as his plane flew away, I drove back to post and headed straight for his old room.

When I got back to the barracks, I saw that his old roommate was cleaning. I looked around and didn't see the teeth anywhere, so I asked the roommate if he had seen the teeth. He told me he had thrown the teeth in the trashcan along with the rest of the stuff the soldier had left behind. When I asked him why he'd done that, he said, "That bastard was such a nasty shit that I had to throw everything away." I went and looked in the trashcan to see if I could find the teeth, but as everything looked so disgusting and damp, I didn't look too long.

I wrote the soldier a letter and included his twenty dollars and explained what had happened. About a month later, he called me from the States, rather pissed, and said he was going to fly back to Germany just to beat the crap out of his old roommate. I told him that for the price of the plane ticket he probably could buy several sets of dentures. That seemed to take some of the wind out of his sails, but he was still adamant about seeking some sort of revenge "for the principle of the matter." He never showed up back in Germany, so I reckon he eventually got over the loss.

THE COUNTRY BOY

ANOTHER WINNER I KNEW WHEN I WAS IN GERMANY WAS THIS LARGE country boy. His claim to fame is that he probably made the promotion to SPC more times in one year than anyone else I've ever known; at least four times in one year, he was promoted, busted, then promoted again. He also was an exceptional mechanic. He could sit down with an operator, and just by how the operator described the problem, he'd have a good idea where to start looking for the problem. He used all his senses to figure out the problem too: sight, smell, sound, touch, and even taste. One time I saw him take a taste of antifreeze to check for traces of oil, or so he claimed; I was in no position to dispute it.

He was what we refer to in the army as "country strong." I remember this one time when I was changing out an M113's final drive, which weighed about four hundred pounds, and I was struggling to hold the part in place while getting the bolts' holes to line up. This mechanic walked up and told me to "get the hell out of the way." Like a good little soldier, I got out of his way. He took the final drive and with one hand held it in place while he tightened the bolts with the other. I was amazed.

For all his good qualities, this mechanic had his demons. He had recently been promoted to Specialist when he was sent to the battalion headquarters to recover a vehicle which wouldn't start. After he had tied on to the vehicle as he began to drive away he had a cigarette hanging out of his mouth., the Command Sergeant Major ran up to the vehicle and yelled, "You're not supposed to smoke cigarettes in military vehicles!" The mechanic answered, "Aw, Sergeant Major, they don't enforce that around here." He then kicked the wrecker into high gear, and the CSM had to jump clear. He lost a stripe for that.

Several months later he was once again promoted to specialist and this time he was working in the motor pool, and we had some cadet lieutenants (CTLTs) working for our unit. The BMO had put one of the CTLTs in charge of putting together a safety board. This CTLT took the job seriously and was looking for some help in getting it set up just right. Now the way one distinguishes a CTLT from a real lieutenant (LT) is the rank on the hat and blouse. The CTLT's rank is nothing more than a round disk, and the regular LT's rank is a gold or silver bar. As this CTLT was asking around for help, he looked to the mechanic. The mechanic looked at the CTLT rather quizzically and stated, "A dot? What the hell is a dot? I don't listen to dots," and then he slowly strolled away. The CTLT was rather dismayed because the battalion commander and the BMO had told him that all the enlisted soldiers would treat him as an officer. Rather peeved, he walked up to the motor sergeant to report the insubordination. The motor sergeant replied, "That mechanic is a country boy. You have to ask him nicely."

Several months later he was once again promoted to Specialist. One Saturday night the mechanic was in his room playing his music rather loudly. The staff-duty officer, while doing his security checks, walked by the mechanic's room, and after he banged on the door for five to ten minutes, the mechanic finally opened it. The staff-duty officer informed the mechanic that he was in violation of the noise ordinance, and he was to turn the music down at once or be reported. The mechanic smirked and slammed the door. The LT, ticked off by now, hustled down to the staff-duty desk and asked the staff-duty NCO where the master keys to the rooms were. The NCO politely showed the LT where the keys were and asked the LT if he wanted any help. The LT, thinking he was invincible, told the NCO, "I think I can handle it." The LT then hustled back up to the mechanic's room and let himself into the room.

I don't know exactly what transpired in the room, as I wasn't there, but about two minutes later, a wall locker came crashing out of the window with the LT inside it. The LT wasn't seriously hurt, just a little disoriented for a couple of days. The chain of command wanted to throw the book at the mechanic, kick him out of the army, and even a little jail time for this assault. Fortunately, for the mechanic, the BMT and the BMS loved him because he was such a gifted mechanic. They were able to convince the chain of command to limit their reaction to non-judicial punishment… basically, he lost another stripe. As you have probably guessed, several months later he was promoted to specialist again.

KIDNAPPING?

I HAVE ONE LAST STORY ABOUT THIS "COUNTRY BOY" MECHANIC. YOU SEE, he was a first-generation native born in the United States. His parents had emigrated from Germany before he was born. He was the oldest child in his family and, as far as I knew, only had one younger sister. I knew he had some first cousins still in Germany and visited them from time to time.

One summer his little sister, who was sixteen at the time, decided she wanted to visit her cousins in Germany and at the same time visit her older brother. She had brought along a friend (who also was about sixteen) for company when she visited her brother. This mechanic, like all the other ones I knew, liked to work hard and party even harder. Before too long the girls were too drunk to be fun anymore, but this mechanic decided he wanted to party some more.

Now, this mechanic had a dilemma on his hands, he didn't want to drag two drunken teenagers around with him all night and he also didn't want to leave these drunken girls in the barracks overnight (that thought makes most fathers cringe). So he did what he thought was the best thing to do, he locked the two girls in his wall locker and headed off to the nearby town of Fulda.

This all transpired on a Friday night.

This mechanic, as stated earlier, was a party animal. He made it a regular habit to head to Fulda and party all weekend, showing back up to post about thirty minutes before PT formation Monday morning. He had just enough time to change into his PT clothes and hustle out the door for formation. This time, when he showed up, things were a bit different. See, he had forgotten he had locked the girls in his wall locker and was being charged with kidnapping.

The girls, it seemed, had woken up inside the wall locker and couldn't recall how they ended up there. They ended up banging on the door and screaming at the top of their voices in an attempt to get someone's attention. As it was a Saturday morning when they woke up, the barracks was for the most part deserted. It must have been hell for them as those wall lockers weren't all that large and I'm sure they both were hung over something fierce.

Eventually the girls were able to gain the attention of someone walking by the room who ran down to the Staff Duty NCO who had access to all the spare keys to the barracks rooms. The girls were rescued and an all-points bulletin was put out looking for the mechanic. When the mechanic showed up early Monday morning there was a note on his door for him to report to the Staff Duty NCO.

The kidnapping charges were dropped and ultimately he ended up losing a stripe. I'm not really sure what he was charged with—my best guess would be general jackassery; but hell, that's why the army has lawyers.

ISSUES IN HOUSING

THE APARTMENT COMPLEX I LIVED AT THE TIME WAS REGARDED TO AS THE "stairwells." This, in and of itself, is not very interesting. What was interesting about my apartment was who lived below me—an NCO who worked in my motor pool. Again this in unremarkable, except this particular NCO was married to a woman who must have been hard of hearing. It is possible, since she was rather large (she must have dressed out to at least a deuce or deuce and a half), that the fat was clogging her ear canals. Not only was she as large as the house she lived in, but she also had one of those personalities that made me want to punch her in the forehead. She also liked to listen to her music rather loudly and at all hours of the day and night. The building I lived in had an inactive building manager to whom I had complained several times about the loud music and, like I suspected, did nothing. I also had talked to the NCO a time or two but was told to mind my own business.

One bright and sunny Saturday morning, while the NCO's large hard-of-hearing wife was blasting her music, I'd had enough. My kids were trying to take their nap, but with the loud music vibrating through the floors, they were having difficulty falling asleep. So I went downstairs and knocked on the door for a couple of minutes, but no one answered. I went back upstairs and called the military police (MP's) and made a noise-ordinance complaint. About five minutes later, the MPs showed up and knocked on the door until the NCO's wife decided to answer. When she did they issued her a noise-ordinance citation.

Not a week later, I arrived home from the field at roughly 0200 hours. As I was putting away my field gear, my Kevlar helmet slipped out of my hands and clunked to the floor. I silently swore and picked it up. About twenty minutes later, I crawled into bed after a quick shower. There was a knock on the door, and I stumbled in the dark to answer it. It was the MP's, who said there was a complaint from the folks downstairs about my banging on the floor. I explained to the MP's that I had just come home from the field and accidently dropped my helmet on the floor, and that must have been what the neighbors were complaining about. The MP's looked at each other then must have decided I really hadn't done anything wrong, so they left.

A couple of days later, the building manager approached me and asked me what I had done to piss off the neighbors below, as the large hard-of-hearing wife was complaining because my dog's nails were making too much noise when they struck the floor. She was threatening to report me again to the MP's. I thought that perhaps she wasn't as hard of hearing as I'd suspected and that maybe the fat was acting as a sound conductor. I also thought her complaint was bordering on ridiculous. I never have understood what went through the mind of that woman.

One bright and early Monday morning, the NCO confronted me (away from prying eyes) and told me what he was going to do to me because I had "gotten him into trouble" with the MP's. He had me pinned against the wall and was glaring at me in an attempt to punk me out. I pushed him away and barked back loudly enough so that some passersby looked down the hallway, wondering what was going on. This NCO was rather larger than I was, and although I don't consider myself a coward, he was rather intimidating. Fortunately, the BMT was walking by and stepped into the hallway. "What the hell is going on here?" he asked.

The NCO said, "Sir, nothing I can't handle." The BMT told the NCO to step into his office and told me to carry on. I have no idea what the BMT did or who he called, but from that point on, the NCO turned a little green every time he looked at me. His wife also never played her music again as far as I knew. The NCO was transferred out a couple of months later.

NEWBEE TRICKS

YEARS EARLIER, WHEN I WAS IN BASIC TRAINING, ONE OF THE FIRST JOKES I was introduced to in the army was one my drill sergeant used on us. He would ask, "What kind of bee's don't sting?"

And we were supposed to respond in unison, "NEWBEES!"

Years later, after I'd been with the battalion for a couple of years, the BMT approached me and told me I was going to start working in the shop office rather than stay on the maintenance bay floor as a mechanic. At first I was rather ticked off about the transfer, but one of the more experienced NCOs pulled me aside and explained to me the reason for the transfer. Apparently the BMT had taken a shine to me for one reason or another and thought I should consider putting my packet in for warrant officer school. The BMT wanted me to get some good experience working in a shop office so as to broaden my knowledge base.

Now, I'm not sure if this guy was telling me the whole truth or not, but I bought it because it was either that or the fact that the maintenance shop was so critically short on personnel and I really sucked as a mechanic. I'd like to think that I was a pretty good mechanic. Rarely did I make a mistake and I was pretty good at this troubleshooting thing. Whatever the reason, I found myself working in the PLL office–or the maintenance shop office. PLL means, Proscribed Load List, I have no idea why it is called "proscribed load list" but the shop is the head shop office where the mechanics get their parts, where the operational status of the vehicles is tracked, and where a soldier goes to dispatch a vehicle. I really don't know why the army decides to call things with such jacked up names. I mean, who thought up PLL? Why not just call it the "shop office"? Just plain silly.

Anyways, not soon after I found myself in the PLL office I met the dumbest kid I've ever known (who wasn't medically diagnosed as "mentally challenged," that is). This knuckleheaded soldier was the kind of soldier who'd ask his sergeant, "What time is the fifteen hundred formation?" One time the shop got the mission to provide one soldier for a range detail, which is normally a rather monotonous detail in which a soldier assists the range officer in charge (OIC) and the noncommissioned officer in charge (NCOIC) with setting up and tearing down a range. The sergeant in charge of my shop selected this knucklehead soldier for this particular detail.

As I was the senior enlisted soldier assigned to the section, this soldier asked me what was required for a person detailed to the range. Wanting to have a little fun with him, I told him his job would be with the "pop-up" portion of the range. He needed to work on his abdominal muscles, as he was to hold a "pop-up" target, lie out in the range, and when given the signal, perform a sit-up and raise the target high over his head. I also informed him he was to ensure the sandbags in front of his area were reinforced so he wouldn't be in danger of a low shot. For the next three days, I noticed this soldier doing sit-ups every chance he got, until the motor sergeant saw him and asked him what he was doing. When the soldier gleefully told him what I had explained to him, the motor sergeant smirked and told him to carry on. The motor sergeant then approached me and said I was to report to him as soon as possible. For the next three weeks, every time I saw the motor sergeant, I was to execute fifty sit-ups on the spot. So much for messing with the dumb guy.

Did I learn my lesson? No, not really. I just found new ways to mess with this guy without the NCOs finding out. I was successful most of the time but this one prank went a little too far. You see, we sent him around to find a box of grid squares. Let me explain the prank for those not in the know. On a topographical map—the type of map the army is in love with—the depicted area is divided into little squares scaled to represent a thousand meters squared or one kilometer squared. These are known as "grid squares." The joke is to send the new guy around to different sections in a vain effort to find grid squares so a map reading class can be given. Generally speaking, a new kid will walk around to a couple of different sections looking for a box of grid squares and eventually, the soldier will either figure out the joke or someone will take pity on the soldier and let them in on the joke. Unfortunately, this was one of those tricks that went a little too far. He was sent from section to section looking for this box of grid squares, and each new contact sent him to another shop.

Eventually this knucklehead was sent to the command sergeant major (CSM, the top noncommissioned officer in a battalion, a very powerful man) for the box of grid squares. The CSM asked him who had started this wild goose chase. This soldier, being dumb but honest, said, "SPC Jones in the motor pool." I got a call to report to the CSM but honestly had forgotten all about the prank. The CSM had me sit down and cut up a stack of old maps into little grid squares. I did this, on my own time, until I had a twelve-by-twelve-by-twelve box filled with grid squares. The CSM told me to give the box to that poor soldier with his compliments. Some pranks end up biting you in the ass.

THE LATRINE AND ME

WORKING IN THE PLL OFFICE WASN'T ALL THAT TAXING. I STILL YEARNED to work on the maintenance floor as a mechanic. When the battalion commander's driver received orders and left the battalion, this left his position vacant. Since the battalion commander preferred to have mechanics as his drivers, I thought this was my chance to get out of the PLL office. So I volunteered. In reality, instead of just being the battalion commander's driver, the motor sergeant decided I was capable of doing both jobs. So the driving thing became more or less an additional duty. A most time consuming additional duty.

The only real trouble with being the commander's driver is you have to drive...everywhere. During the year I spent as his driver, I must have put 150,000 miles on his vehicles. The commander had two vehicles. One was a TMP van[8], and the other was a HMMWV. We drove the HMMWV more in the local training areas and the van more when we had to drive between training areas.

On one particular trip, we'd been driving nonstop for about six hours (the man had an iron bladder). We were in Hohenfels, the largest training area in Germany at that time, and he had to go to a meeting in Albertshof, the garrison location in Hohenfels. To be blunt, I had to take a crap so badly that my eyes were watering. I didn't want to exceed the posted speed limit, as the MPs would love to pull over a battalion commander, and to get pulled over was a quick way to get fired.

I pulled up to the building where the commander had his meeting. I explained my situation, and he said he would be several hours, so I had time to drive to the nearest latrine, take care of my business, then return to pick him up. He jumped out, and I hightailed it to the nearest latrine.

Albertshof was situated in a rectangular shape with roads that ran north-south and east-west, with latrines on the corners of every other

---

8. A green Volkswagen van borrowed from the Post run Temporary Motor Pool

road. All the buildings looked exactly the same, so it was important to keep track of where you were in regard to the latrines. I pulled up in front of the first latrine I found, parked my vehicle, and moved out smartly. I bee-lined it to the first stall, checked to ensure there was toilet paper (a must), and commenced doing my duty.

After the initial blast, things seemed to settle down a bit. I was just about done when I heard light steps in the hallway. Then I heard high-pitched giggling. Oh, shit—I was in a female latrine, and some gals were headed to the showers. This is what I call truly a bad situation.

At this time in the 1990s, if you remember correctly, the army was going through some pretty tough times with regard to gender issues (seems this is an ongoing issue). There were a couple of sergeants major being court-martialed for sexual infidelity; there was that issue out at Aberdeen Proving Ground with the drill sergeants; and the US president himself was experiencing some infidelity issues as well. No one would think twice about busting little ol' me for hanging out in a female latrine, and no one would accept this situation as an innocent mistake, especially my wife.

What was I going to do? I sat there for about thirty minutes and waited for the two girls to finish their showers and walk out of the latrine. By this time my legs had started to fall asleep. That couldn't matter. I had to time this correctly, so I waited, listened, and waited some more. When I was reasonably sure I didn't hear anything, I busted out of the stall and hustled to my HMMWV with my hat pulled down as low as I could get it and my eyes toward the ground.

Fortunately I didn't get stopped, and no one said a word to me, even though there were people all around outside the latrine. I jumped into my HMMWV, started her up, and drove away as if nothing had happened. Thank you, Jesus.

THE PROMOTION BOARD

SOMETIME EARLY IN 1994, I HAD REACHED A POINT AS A SPECIALIST WHERE I needed to go to the promotion board. I need to explain a little about army enlisted promotions before I continue with this story. When a person enlists in the army, most of the time they start out as a private, either as a PV1 or PV2, the difference being the pay grade. If that person has some sort of leadership-type experience, either having been an Eagle Scout, a member of Junior ROTC (high school reserve officer training corps), or ROTC at a college, they get extra stripes, maybe private first class (PFC) or specialist (SPC), the difference being that one is a higher rank than the other, and the higher the rank, the better the pay. The difference in pay is not much really, but it could mean the difference between being able to afford a bottle of Jack Daniels or the bottom shelf "military-special brand whiskey"—truly a "rot gut" whiskey!!.

Before one can get promoted to sergeant (also known as a "noncommissioned officer" or "NCO"), one has to be a good soldier for a specific time period, usually not to exceed thirty-six months. Every month the soldier is supposed to be counseled on paper, with remarks regarding which areas he or she is good to go in and which areas he or she needs to work on in order to be selected to go to a promotion board. When the soldier reaches thirty-six months in service, he or she is either sent to the promotion board or a counseling statement must be written to the soldier that explains why he or she isn't being recommended to the promotion board.

Every month prior to my thirty-sixth month, I either hadn't received a counseling statement or had received one stating that I was a great soldier and would make a good NCO. I was sure I was going to the board at my thirty-sixth-month mark and would do great at it. At the time I was still working in the PLL shop and even though I wasn't an MOS-trained PLL clerk but a mechanic, I was given responsibility over the largest company in the battalion, and I also was the battalion commander's driver[9]. I also had the ear of the BMT. With all this going for me in my life at this time, I knew I was a shoo-in for the promotion board.

During the month of December, 1993, the battalion commander had to go to the field a lot, and as I was his driver, I was in the field as well. We were gone almost twenty-nine of the thirty-one days in December. In January, around the first of the month, I received a counseling statement that stated that I would go to the board in February. I was as happy as a fat cat. I went home and told my wife, who was, as always, my biggest supporter.

A little side note here—when a soldier goes to the promotion board, the first sergeants and the command sergeant major of the battalion test the soldier on his or her knowledge of the army, and they assess whether the soldier would make a fit-to-fight NCO. This is a rather subjective process, and almost everyone who goes before the board passes. During all my years in the army, I've heard of only a handful of soldiers who didn't pass the board.

Back in the day, before the Internet, cell phones, and the Information Age, if a soldier wanted to study for the board, he or she had to find the army manuals and read them; I did this with my wife. We'd read the manuals together, and then she'd ask me questions from the manual to test my retention. As she is significantly smarter than I am, she always retained more knowledge than I did; perhaps she should have gone to the board. Years later, when I was a platoon leader (also known as a "PL," a first or second lieutenant who leads a platoon), with all this knowledge in my wife's melon, there were several times when a first sergeant or two would call her and ask her for a reference. I always found this fact rather funny—my wife, the expert on the army. But I digress.

My wife and I had been studying on and off for several months, so I had a pretty good grasp of the army and its ways. At the promotion board, a soldier reports while wearing class As, which are just about the most worthless of all army uniforms. Prior to the 1990s, all soldiers traveled in their class As, so it made sense to keep them looking good and to present a professional look for the army. Sometime in the 1990s, soldiers became targets for terrorists, and a good way to identify a soldier while he or she was traveling was to look for a class A uniform. After these attacks

9. A position of great responsibility as the battalion commander's vehicle had better not be inoperable at any time

began—although I can't say I've ever heard of such an attack, but that's the reasoning I've heard—the policy became for soldiers to wear civilian clothes while traveling. Subsequently the class A uniform was of little or no use except for inspections or boards. I wanted my class As to look sharp for my board, so I planned to wait until the last possible moment to have them cleaned and altered.

Shortly after I received my counseling for the month of December, the battalion commander had to go to the field again, which meant I had to go as well. We'd be back with plenty of time for me to have my class As cleaned and altered. The battalion commander and I got out of the field with about a week or so before the board. I was really excited because the promotion board was taking place on a Friday. I went to work the Monday before the board and was expecting my NCO to provide me with a memorandum explaining all the things I needed to do to prepare for the board. The memo was a formal affair, and truthfully, it provided only two things for the soldier—one, confirmation of going to the board; and two, the areas required for study. Although everything about the army was testable, this memo offered specifics. I needed to know everything, but if I wanted to be squared away, I needed to know these particular subjects. I received no such memo. I knew the memos were out, because a friend of mine was going to the same board, and he had received one, so I asked my NCO why I hadn't gotten one. He told me that he had forgotten to submit my name to the first sergeant and that I needed to wait until March. This more or less got my dander up. You see, January was my thirty-sixth month in the army. I had been, more or less on paper, a squared-away[10] soldier. I was being screwed. I told my NCO that, and I also told him it was my thirty-sixth month in the army, and if he wasn't sending me, I wanted to know why, and "I forgot" was a bullshit answer.

He then told me my job performance in the shop had slipped lately, and he was ticked that he had to cover down[11] on my work. I told him that answer was bullshit, because for fifty of the last sixty days, I had been in the field and hadn't been in the office long enough to square my computer away[12]. When I'd been selected to be the battalion commander's

---

10. An army term meaning "great"
11. To cover down on someone's work means to do their work for them
12. Another use of the term "squared away"—it can be used for things as well as people

driver, he'd agreed to spread some of the workload around during the times when I had to drive the battalion commander around.

During this same meeting, he wrote a negative counseling statement about my job performance, which I refused to sign. I left the office and went to smoke a cigarette. While I was outside, I got word that the battalion commander wanted to see me. Over the past two months or so, I had driven him more than fifteen hundred miles in the field, never had a breakdown, and never had gotten stuck, and he never had to wait for anything. He was going to "coin me" for being such a good driver. The commander's coin has a long history in the army. Originally it was meant as a "three-day pass" or as a "get out of jail free" award for small infractions. For example, if a soldier did a good thing, he or she would get a coin; if he or she showed up late or made some other little infraction, the soldier could give the coin back, and everything would be "even." The battalion commander had told me that in his twenty-year career I was the best driver he'd ever had. I wasn't feeling so good at the time, however, as just about everything I'd worked for was crashing before my eyes.

I dragged my butt up to the battalion commander's office. I must have had a whipped-dog look on my face when I arrived, because after he gave me the coin, he asked me what was wrong. I told him what had just transpired, and he agreed it was bullshit. He then called in the battalion command sergeant major (BN CSM) and asked him to look into the matter. At this point I'll bet if there are any old-school NCOs out there, they'll know how the BN CSM felt. For those of you who don't know much about the army, there's a thing called "NCO business." This is business, NCOs feel, that officers have no business getting involved with. It would have been better for me to piss on a Bible in front of the chaplain than to get the BN Commander involved with the promotion board. Of course the BN CSM said, "Yes, sir!" but he probably was thinking, *I'll get you* [meaning me], *you little shit.* I more or less knew I was in trouble. I didn't get my memorandum to report to the board until Thursday afternoon. Typically a soldier is given the day off prior to the board in order to prepare. That night I worked until 2300 hours and had worked late every night that week. I was told I had to make up all the work I had missed while in the field before I could go home.

As I was going home, I remembered I'd forgotten to drop my class As off at the alterations shop. I figured I was screwed anyway, so what difference did it make? When I got home, I must have looked like hell.

My wife, my biggest supporter, knew what was happening. She had taken my class As to the cleaners for me, but I still needed them altered a little. I looked in a mirror and realized I needed a haircut badly. Although I wasn't out of regulation, when you go to the board, it's always better to have a fresh haircut. My morale was pretty much in the dumps.

My wife, God bless her, told me to "suck it up and drive on." She never had seen me quit anything in my life, and she wasn't about to let me quit now. We were going to show those pricks that they couldn't keep a good soldier down. She brewed a hot pot of strong coffee, grabbed a set of clippers, sat me down, and gave me the best haircut I've ever had. She then set out my class As and showed what a whiz she was with duct tape and staples. All the while she quizzed me on all the army subjects we had studied together. We didn't go to bed that night. The next morning, when I left the house, I felt like a million dollars.

When I arrived at the board, I began to get nervous again. All the people who hated me at that moment were gathering around, and I knew my fate was sealed. I kept thinking about my wife. I wouldn't let her down; I wouldn't let myself down. Usually those going before the board go in alphabetical order. This time that wasn't the case. I mean, I did go to school in Texas, so I knew I had the forty-sixth best education in the United States, and I was sure with a name like "Jones" I should have gone in closer to the beginning, but for some reason, I was selected to go last. I was sure they were going to hang me and dump my body in a trashcan somewhere. Somewhere in the back of my mind, I began to look for a place to escape. All the other soldiers had finished, and I was about to be called in.

Finally the door opened. Everything seemed to be moving in slow motion. My heart thumped as the adrenalin flowed through my veins. Fight or flight? Fight or flight? I decided to fight.

Just then a van pulled up in front of the building. A medium-size man climbed out and hustled inside. I recognized him as the division CSM. He told me to stand fast[13], which I did. The division CSM walked into the boardroom, sat down, and told the BN CSM, "I'm taking over your board." As if I weren't nervous enough, now the most powerful (enlisted) man in the division was sitting on my board. I knew I was screwed.

---

13. "Standing fast" is another one of those army terms that civilians have a hard time understanding. To "stand fast" means to stand still. I don't know where it originated, but that's what it means.

Holy shit—my infraction of the "enlisted code" had gone outside of the battalion. They were really out for blood.

The door opened again, and I heard, "Hey, knucklehead. Get your butt in here." I moved out smartly and reported to the board. They made me do facing movements, and I executed them flawlessly. At any moment I expected one of the first sergeants to jump across the table and strangle me. After I finished my facing movements, I stood there nervously facing the board. It was time for the questions. My wife and I had studied for this moment for close to a year. I knew I couldn't remember all the answers to all the possible questions, so I'd memorized the numbers and titles of all the field manuals (FMs), technical manuals (TMs), and training circulars (TCs). I figured if I didn't remember the answer to the question, I could always reference the manual. For example if I were asked, "Soldier, explain to me in detail how to dress a gunshot wound," my answer would be, "First Sergeant, I fail to remember the proper procedures to dress a gunshot wound. I will reference FM 21-11 [medical procedures] and get you the answer in the morning, First Sergeant!"[14] This was my plan.

The first question was, "Soldier, what's the method of building a directional antenna if you don't have an OE-254 at your disposal!" Uh, I hadn't covered that during my studies. I mean, who would? I knew of a communications manual, but I was sure it didn't cover "directional antennas." I had no idea how to answer this. Then the division CSM shouted, "First Sergeant, I don't see that question outlined on the MOI [memorandum of instruction, the memo stating which questions the first sergeants were to use so that all the soldiers being tested would be tested on the same material]. You need to restate your question." I thought, *Wow, that was a surprise.*

The division CSM must have seen the frustration on my face, and he told me in a calm voice, "Son, you need to relax a little. At ease and breathe." I began to relax.

The first sergeant asked his question. I truthfully don't remember what all the questions were. I mean, that was more than fifteen years ago, but I remember that every time a first sergeant tried to deviate from the MOI, the division CSM crushed his balls. When the board was finally over, the division CSM asked me, "Son, do you have anything else to say?" I thought for a moment then said, "CSM, I may not know everything there is to know about the army, but if you give me a mission, consider

---

14. You always answer a question with, "First Sergeant, blah blah blah, First Sergeant!"

it complete, CSM!" With that I saluted the board members and walked out smartly.

Out of a possible two hundred points, I scored 186, the highest for the day. Back in those days, I'd only heard of one other soldier ever scoring higher. The guy who had scored higher had a photographic memory and liked to read military manuals, which is kind of like licking sandpaper. I think he scored 187.

Monday morning, when I got to work, I received a message that the operations sergeant major (SGM; a CSM is the highest in a battalion or brigade, while an SGM is of the same pay grade but is a lower position) wanted to see me. I knew who the operations SGM was but had few dealings with him in the past. I reported to him, and he asked, "How was your board?" He asked the question in a way that made me believe he already knew and was just checking on me. He sat me down to explain. He told me that on Thursday night before the board he had overheard the CSM and the first sergeants plotting how they were going to screw me. Therefore he called the division CSM. Apparently the division CSM had been the operations SGM's section chief back in the day. They had pretty much followed each other around the world, always keeping tabs on each other.

I was shocked. I asked him why he was willing to help me, as I didn't know him all that well. He told me he knew a good soldier when he saw one. He also said I was the best mechanic he'd seen in a long while. He reminded me of a time, about a year ago or so, when his tracked vehicle had broken down in the field. The first mechanic had stopped by and told him his tracked vehicle wasn't going to be operational for some time. At the time I had just started driving for the battalion commander, and we had arrived near the SGM's tracked vehicle. The operations sergeant remembered my stopping to chat with another mechanic, and I had overheard about the track being down. He said he remembered my walking up to the engine compartment, and with nothing more than a pocket knife, a piece of wire, and some tape, I had bypassed whatever it was that was broken, and the track ran beautifully from that point forward.

This led me to think you always have one more friend than you think you have. As to what happened to the BN CSM and the first sergeants? I'm not sure. I know they weren't around the battalion for very long after that. I think they were "retired."

Not too long after the board, I received PCS (Permanent Change of Station)[15] orders to move to Fort Carson, Colorado. Several of my buddies in Germany told me how lucky I was to be moving to Fort Carson, as it was a beautiful post with lots of family things to do. I never should have listened to them.

*The truth behind this story is, well, it boils down to the actual CSM in control of the board. In reality, it wasn't the division CSM, it was the battalion CSM. The truth is it was the 1SGs who were plotting against me, not the CSM with the 1SGs. The Operations SGM did overhear the 1SGs plotting and instead of going straight to the Division CSM he went to the battalion CSM. He did threaten to call the division CSM though. I changed the story because the division CSM at the time was CSM (R) Tilley. I really respect that man and all he stands for. I wanted to give him some credit so I changed that aspect of the story.

As a side note, there was this one time I was placed on KP (Kitchen Police)[16] while in Hoenfels. Normally it was a big "no no" to put your mechanics on KP because there was a theater-wide shortage of mechanics. We were essentially duty free (no KP, no CQ (Charge of Quarters), no staff duty, etc. and we were generally worked from 0600 to 2000 with the exception of Thursdays (family time at 1500 was sacred). CSM Tilley showed up and was visiting with those of us on KP. He was asking us where we were from and what we did in the army. When he asked me and I told him I was a mechanic, he pretty much flipped out on my chain of command. You know, "If you have enough mechanics to put them on KP and out of the motor pool then I guess you don't need any more...."

I was replaced within 15 minutes. It wasn't that I minded being on KP, hell I'll do just about anything required of me, it was just that I had vehicles to fix and my job as a mechanic didn't stop just because I was on KP. Being on KP just added more to my plate. I was looking at pulling an all-nighter working on vehicles even before they put me on KP.

Months later, while at the battalion ball, CSM Tilley remembered me and asked if the chain of command had abused me since. They hadn't to that point. The ball was about two months before the board incident. I like to think CSM Tilley, had he known about the little 1SG plot, would have reacted like I illustrate in this story. Just my little way of paying tribute to a man I think of as the epitome of an NCO.

15. To PCS is to move from one post or base to another. In the 90's a married Soldier could expect to move about every three years and an unmarried one about every two years.
16. Augmentee to the cooks

IN-PROCESSING
AT FORT CARSON

SEVERAL MONTHS LATER I RECEIVED ORDERS TO PCS TO FORT CARSON, Colorado. At first I was rather excited because Fort Carson was located near Colorado Springs, Colorado and it was known for outdoors activities like hunting, fishing, skiing, etc. My experience there fell short of my expectations. My experience at Fort Carson was one of misery and poverty. When I lived in Germany, the army had given me a furnished house and paid all the utility bills (except the phone bill, which, if properly managed, could run less than $50 a month). I also lived within walking distance of my place of work, so although I had a car, I didn't really need it. During the three years I lived in Germany, I put maybe 6,000 miles total on the three different cars I had. At Fort Carson I put that many miles on my car in about three months. We didn't get paid very well back then, and there surely wasn't this thing called a "variable housing allowance," so a soldier had to pay out of pocket to make up for shortages for the expense of living in an area where apartments cost an arm and a leg. I was paying more rent for my nine-hundred–square-foot apartment in Fort Carson in 1994 than I did for my house at Fort Sill in 1998. More than half my paycheck went to paying the bills just to live while at Fort Carson. Lucky, huh?

When I first arrived at Fort Carson, there was a rather sensible in-processing procedure that was developed by the post commander at that time. This is no bullshit; it was a rather airtight plan that really made sense. When a soldier arrived at Fort Carson, he or she was immediately assigned to a unit, but the soldier was retained at the replacement detachment (repo depot) until all required classes, equipment draws, or whatever had to be done was done, so that when a soldier arrived at the final unit, he or she was a fully trained, deployable soldier. Makes sense, right? This process usually took about two weeks. I arrived at the post, went to the repo depot, and signed in. Then I received my in-brief (which more or less explained the process above), was assigned a room and a roommate, and then was told to report back the next morning when all this great in-processing would start. As a side note, my wife and kids were visiting my parents and the plan was for them to stay there until I secured housing.

I met my roommate, a nice fellow, and he and I agreed that after we got our room situated, we'd grab a bite to eat. We had just finished with the room and were headed downstairs when I heard over the intercom, "SPC Jones report to the front desk." Like any good soldier would, I detoured and headed for the front desk. When I got there, I was introduced to my new motor sergeant, who told me to go grab my bags, as I was going to the field that night. I ran upstairs, grabbed my bags (I didn't have time for it to sink in yet that I was being screwed over), went outside, and saw a HMMWV with a toolbox laid out in the back. That night I worked in the motor pool until after midnight. Staying in the motor pool was "going to the field," I reckon.

At Fort Carson, around that time, there was a standing order by the commanding general (CG) that no soldier was to work past 1700 hours on a normal-duty day (1500 on Thursdays, which I'll explain later), unless it had been briefed on the training schedule six weeks prior. My unit was the exception to that policy. To explain, I'll have to get into a little of what the army calls "busted fleet." For a given unit, there are X number of vehicles of each type. Some are what are referred to as "pacing items." A pacing item is that one piece of equipment or vehicle type that is vital for that specific unit's mission. One takes the number of vehicles assigned to a given unit (by type) and multiplies it by the number of days in a given month in order to come up with "possible available days." For example, 9 M1059s (SMK GEN VEH) x 30 = 270. Now we've determined there are 270 possible available days in a month for this vehicle type. If a unit has any one or a multiple number of those vehicles down for more than 10 percent of the possible available days (for example, 10 percent of 270 = 27), then that unit has "busted fleet" for that vehicle type. This is a bad thing. The pacing item for my unit at Fort Carson was the M1059. We only had nine in the entire division, so when one went down for maintenance it was "balls to the wall" to get it operational. Hence my commander was authorized to work his mechanics late to fix these vehicles (or anything else that needed doing, as long as he could justify to his boss that we were working on the

M1059s). I don't think I ate dinner with my family or did PT for most of that year. I typically got home after 2100 hours and had to be in the motor pool before 0600. Lots of fun.

At any rate, there I was, in this unit that hadn't only the ability to abuse mechanics but also an inborn desire to do so, or so it seemed. Because I hadn't gone through in-processing at the repo depot, I didn't have any field gear except what I personally had bought. During this time period in the army, Thursday mornings were sacred. Formation was generally at 0700; the uniform was field gear; and the mission was sergeants' time (time allotted to the NCOs to train their soldiers without having to deal with training distractions). Sergeants' time lasted until 1200 hours, at which time we'd break to eat then regroup at 1300 for "crew drills" or activities and recreation (A and R). For mechanics, this meant "services in MOPP 4" (Mission Oriented Protective Posture level 4)[17] or "how to troubleshoot…" Basically it meant work. At 1300, while the rest of the company was off conducting crew drills or playing sports, the mechanics were in the motor pool cleaning or servicing stuff.

One thing the commanding general didn't budge on, however, was the "family time," which at Fort Carson was from 1500 until 1800. This meant everyone had to be off the banana belt[18], and if he found someone working, the entire chain of command was to report to his office with an explanation. So typically we mechanics got off at 1500 on Thursdays, but there were times when we had to return to work at 1800 after "family time" to tighten up any loose strings.

So, no shit, there I was, standing in formation for sergeants' time, not in field gear, as I hadn't been issued any. As I mentioned, I hadn't gone through the in-processing procedure, because I'd been pulled out the first day in order to work late. I was now being singled out as the

---

17. MOPP gear is basically Nuclear, Chemical, and Biological (NBC) protective gear designed to allow a soldier to complete his mission in a contaminated environment. The different levels are designated based off of threat. MOPP level 0 is—MOPP gear available not worn. MOPP level 1 is when the soldier wears the coat and trousers (basically a cotton suit with charcoal sewn in as a filter). MOPP level 2 is with rubberized over boots worn. MOPP level 3 is with rubberized gloves worn. And finally, MOPP level 4 is with protective mask worn. MOPP gear is extremely cumbersome and tends to not allow the body to cool itself so sweat pools in just about every place sweat can pool. After wearing MOPP gear for 30 minutes or so you feel as if you've taken a sweat bath. Not a fun time…

18. The motor-pool road at Fort Carson was called the "banana belt," because it was basically shaped like a banana—lots of imagination there.

dipshit who'd forgotten about sergeants' time because I wasn't wearing field gear. The first couple of times, it didn't really bother me. Six months later, still explaining to the platoon sergeant why I didn't have my field gear, however, did get rather annoying (as if it were my fault). See, in order to get issued the field gear outside of the repo depot, a soldier had to have a memorandum signed by the company commander explaining why the soldier didn't have his gear. The company commander wasn't willing to sign this memo, because he didn't want to explain anything, so I continued to be the dipshit who'd forgotten about that most sacred of practices—field gear and sergeants' time.

Several months later, I ran into a NCO who looked familiar. I approached him, and no shit, he had been a PV2 I knew from Germany. He had been promoted to PFC, and not long after I went to the board and became "promotable"—meaning I'd met all the qualifications for promotion and just needed to make points. I'd normally explain the promotion point system to the reader, but it's really too convoluted, and I believe anyone who claims to understand it is not really telling the truth. Anyways, this PFC got caught smoking dope and was busted back to PV2. Now, about fifteen months later, I ran into him at Fort Carson, and he was sporting sergeant stripes. And, because the army promotion system is rather screwed up, his dope-smokin' ass could not only make his rank back but also could get promoted ahead of folks like me who never really had done anything too wrong. Bullshit, huh?

Another month or two passed, and everything was chugging along when one of my mechanic buddies ETS'ed out of the army. He had this highfalutin' idea of becoming a masseuse and earning, in his words, "shitloads of money." Apparently his idea was somewhat faulty, as a month later he was caught in the barracks, sleeping in one of his buddies' rooms. He was also eating in the chow hall on an ID card he had "lost" while on active duty. He was unceremoniously escorted off the post and told not to return.

Around this time, the company headed to the field. I still didn't have any field gear and received no less than three ass chewin's as a result, but by now my rear was getting rather pockmarked and tough, so the ass chewin' rolled off me like water on a duck's back. I drove the recovery tracked vehicle to the field, set up in the perimeter, and took to manning the .50 cal. One cool thing about this .50 cal was that it had a night sight on it. With fresh batteries I could see probably a half mile or farther at night.

I've always been told that light can travel at night as far as the eye can see. I know most of you are thinking, *Yeah, that's about two cans of "no shit," Jones*, but I swear I never really believed it until I saw it for myself while pulling security this night. I looked out across the way and saw a faint glow. I couldn't really tell what it was, but I knew I saw it. I raised the .50 cal and peered at the glow through the scope and saw three guys sitting on the hood of a HMMWV smoking cigarettes. Based on a quick analysis with a map, I estimated they were about a half mile away. I reported what I saw to the sergeant of the guard. The fellas sitting on the hood of the HMMWV were "OPFOR"[19] and I was given credit for a "Kill" that night. During a field exercise we can't shoot real bullets at each other. Sometimes we are able to use "MILES gear" (an older not so user-friendly laser tag system) but this time I didn't have MILES gear. So I "notionally" killed the opposing forces.

We were in the field for about a week or so. As soon as we got back, we did a quick wash of our vehicles and headed to the house. This particular weekend, the commander decided to give us an extra day off, so we reported back on Tuesday rather than Monday. When we arrived I fell into formation, and the fella standing next to me smelled rather ripe. I looked over and recognized the NCOIC of the recovery tracked vehicle. He smiled at me, and I saw he had green teeth, which almost made me puke right then and there. I noticed he still had dirt on his arms, which had been there the week prior. I asked him if he had taken a shower since we'd been back. He quickly quit smiling and told me to mind my own business. I made sure I was in front of him during the run—he really smelled terrible.

---

19. OPFOR stands for "Opposing Forces" or the fellas selected to act as the "bad guys."

FAT MEN CAN FLY

AT FORT CARSON I WAS ASSIGNED TO WORK WITH A CHEMICAL COMPANY on their M1059's (Smoke Generators). I think I was a rather good mechanic as I never found a problem I couldn't troubleshoot and correct. The challenge I always found working on a tracked vehicle was to try and solve the problem without having to pull the pack. The pack is the engine/transmission/transfer package—they are all connected together and are designed to come out as one piece and then, if need be, the pack is split and the needed component(s) is/are replaced.

This one morning, while I had the engine compartment open and I was in the middle of replacing an oil hose which ran between the engine and transmission that had somehow sprung a leak, I was laying on top of the engine with my arms down in between them turning a wrench about 1/8 of an inch at a time. I had the operator sitting in the driver's seat and her only job was to ensure no one started the engine while I was lying on top of it. It must have been about lunch time because her NCOIC walked up behind the vehicle, the ramp was down, and told her to crank the engine and raise the ramp so they could go to lunch.

I heard her say, "Ok" and the next thing I knew the engine began to turn over. I'll swear, you've never seen a fat man move that fast as I propelled myself about five feet into the air, landing hard on my feet in front of the tracked vehicle. I was yelling at the top of my lungs (and may have slipped in a few expletives as well) as I was flying through the air. "SHUT IT OFF!!! SHUT IT OFF!!!" She had fear in her eyes as she scrambled around for the kill switch. I was shaking all over as my body dealt with the adrenaline flowing through my veins.

I fell backward, hard, sitting on the ground for a minute or two. I could feel the heat buildup under my collar as I became more and more pissed. I mean that stupid soldier only had one job and she failed at it— nearly having my arm ripped off by the rotation of the engine. I think at that point I was the closest I have ever come to wanting to murder someone.

After my heart began to slip from my throat back to where it belonged, I walked around back because I wanted to punch her platoon sergeant in the forehead as hard as I could as well as shove a wrench in that soldier's fourth point of contact (namely her ass). The platoon sergeant must have sensed I was about to inflict some violence on him because he dropped the book he had been carrying and took a step back almost in a posturing position. He looked like he was ready to square off with me. As I approached, I saw the soldier crawl out of the back of the vehicle with a flustered look on her face. Lots of emotions and thoughts raced through my head as I stood there contemplating what to do.

I knew that if I were to deck this NCO, regardless of the cause, the outcome for me wouldn't be pretty. No one had been hurt and punching an NCO is rather taboo. Instead, I sat down and smoked a cigarette and told them both to just leave me alone…with helpers like that I decided from then on not to work with someone sitting in the driver's hatch. I would disconnect the batteries (which I should have done in the first place) and tell everyone to just get the hell away from the vehicle.

ETS

I HAD BEEN IN THIS UNIT FOR ROUGHLY SIX MONTHS WHEN I DECIDED I'D had just about enough of the army and figured out that I wasn't so "lucky" to have been assigned to Fort Carson. When the reenlistment man came around promising all sorts of nice candy if I were to stay in the army, I told him to stick it where the sun don't shine. I was out of there!

To begin the ETS process, a soldier needs a little thing called orders. I had none. A soldier was supposed to receive ETS orders about six months before his or her ETS date. It was going on May 1995, and I had an ETS date of November 1995, so I began to ask, "Where are my orders?" I thought that was a natural question. One month turned into two months, which turned into three—still no orders. Every morning it seemed like I'd approach my platoon sergeant and ask him for help, and I'd get some sort of grumbling reply about my not having field gear (as if one had anything to do with the other).

Around this time, I was scheduled to undergo shoulder surgery (I had fallen off a tracked vehicle sometime in the past, which had caused some extensive damage), and with this surgery came three weeks of convalescent leave. I talked with my platoon sergeant, my first sergeant, and my commander and asked them to help me with my orders, as I still had no intention of reenlisting. They all smiled and told me that when I got back from leave my orders would be waiting for me in the training room. Three weeks went by, and I returned to work—surprise, no orders. At this point things were getting rather ridiculous. I started to develop a bit of a negative attitude toward my superiors, as I was beginning to get the idea they didn't have my best interests in mind. Another month passed before the shit really hit the fan.

It was now October 30, 1995, and my ETS date was November 27, 1995 (roughly twenty-eight days out). I believe it was a Wednesday night, and I was sitting in the motor pool, BS'ing with some of the guys, when my platoon sergeant (PSG) walked in and informed me I was to report to the the staff duty officer and act as the staff-duty runner that night. I informed the PSG that there was a rumor going around that when a soldier had thirty days or less before his ETS date, he or she would be removed from the duty roster. The PSG asked me where that was written, and like all good barracks lawyers, I had no idea. So I picked up the phone and called the inspector general (IG)[20].

The conversation went something like this.

IG: "Good afternoon. IG section. This is MSG So-and-So."

Me: "Hello, I don't want to give my name, as I don't want any repercussions, but is there a regulation or something that states I don't have to pull duty thirty days from my ETS?"

IG: "Yes, it's Fort Carson regulation 210-8."

Me: "Thanks."

I hung up the phone and informed my PSG of the regulation, to which I received the reply, "Shut up, and do as you're told."

I called the IG back, and the conversation went like this.

IG: "Good afternoon. IG section. This is MSG So-and-So."

Me: "Hello, my name is SPC Jones, and I'm with such and such company. My PSG is trying to make me pull staff duty as a driver, and I'm twenty-eight days out from my ETS date."

IG: "Go home tonight, and we'll deal with this in the morning."

So I went home. When I got there, my answering machine was smoking hot with the message the first sergeant had left on it. He used just about every curse word in the book, informed me that my parents weren't married when I was born, and even suggested my mother had four legs, a tail, and howled at the moon. I kept the tape (way back in those days telephone answering machines used tapes rather than digital memory... how things change). The next morning, when I showed up to formation, I was hustled into the training room, where everyone with a stripe on his or her collar gave me the third degree. This culminated with my standing outside the commander's office waiting on his determination regarding my future. I took this opportunity to call MSG So-and-So again. The conversation went something like this.

IG: "Good morning. IG section. This is MSG So-and-So."

Me: "MSG So-and-So, this is SPC Jones again." I then explained my situation.

---

20. The IG is the guy with all the answers in the army; you have to be careful when you contact the IG, because you may just find out you're wrong, too.

IG: "Hold on. I'll be right there. Don't sign anything."

About fifteen minutes later, the MSG came busting through the door with orders assigning me to the IG office. He told the first sergeant he wanted to conduct a pop inspection of all the unit's training records, counseling records, and maintenance records. He explained that a member of the IG staff was going to be at the company area at 0900 to start. He took me aside and told me to go home and report to his office around 0900.

CLEARING POST

WHEN I SHOWED UP AT THE MSG'S OFFICE AT 0845, HE ASKED ME WHAT I needed in the way of help. I explained that first I needed orders so I could start clearing. He told me to go and take care of any business I had to take care of (army lingo for "Go and do anything else…just don't do it here. Or, go and sham while I figure this out"), and I was to report back to his office at 1300. When I showed up at 1300, he had a set of memorandums signed by the CG authorizing me to clear without orders. I then set out about clearing post. I ran into some problems, however, when it came to transportation.

Transportation is where a soldier goes to coordinate his or her household goods for shipment. As this was a turbulent time in the area, 4th Infantry Division was moving to Fort Hood, and 3rd Armored Cavalry Regiment was moving to Fort Carson, there weren't any transportation appointments available within my twenty-seven day window. I had to leave my apartment by November 30, as my rental agreement was up, and to extend it to a "month-to-month" rental was far too expensive for me. At this time in my life, I couldn't have afforded even a storage room as a temporary solution. I told the woman at the transportation office my woes, and her basic reaction was, "It's not my problem." This had me rather down and I didn't know what to do.

I went back to MSG So-and-So's office and sat down. He asked me what was wrong, and when I informed him, he said, "Hang on a minute." He called the transportation woman for me, but he got the same response. He then asked the woman to hold for a moment. He leaned back in his chair and asked his boss, a colonel (COL) infantry type, who apparently had been briefed on my situation, if he would chat with this nice lady. The COL said, "No problem." He picked up the phone and spoke very clearly.

IG: "Ma'am, I'm COL So-and-So. Do you know who I am?"

Trans: "Yes, sir."

IG: "You know who my boss is, right?"

Trans: "Yes, sir."

IG: "Do you want the next call you receive to be from my boss?"

Trans: "No, sir. How does November seventeenth sound?"

The COL looked at me, and I gave him the thumbs-up, as that was a Saturday, and I didn't have any other plans except to get out of there.

The conclusion of this story lies somewhere between truth and speculation. Over time I pieced it together from people I knew there and people I ran into several years later who remember this incident. As I left the post, a wake of destruction swept my unit clean of all wrongdoers and abusers of soldiers. The first sergeant and the company commander were relieved[21]. The battalion commander and CSM both received letters of reprimand[22].

As to how I ended up in the position I was in, well, apparently the first sergeant's wife worked at the repo depot as an assignments NCO (who also was relieved). You see, in those days mechanics were hard to come by, and the company I was assigned to didn't have any to speak of. When I arrived on post, I was gold from a maintenance point of view. The first sergeant's wife had assigned me to her husband's company without anyone of authority knowing about it or approving the assignment (there were other units on post with a higher priority). My paperwork conveniently had been "lost" behind a filing cabinet, so I never had been in-processed. Technically I was absent without leave (AWOL). The big army had no idea where I was or what I was doing, and this is the reason I hadn't received my ETS orders. The big army didn't know where to send them.

---

21. To be relieved in the army is the same as being fired in the civilian world

22. A letter of reprimand is a really bad thing, basically one step shy of being fired and generally a career ender.

CIF

PART OF THE "CLEARING POST" REQUIREMENTS WAS TO TURN IN YOUR gear at the central issuing facility (CIF). As I didn't have any equipment issued, this process was rather easy for me. At most posts at this time, however, clearing CIF was one of the most difficult tasks, and most soldiers dreaded it like a bad hangover.

Now this next story is one that is founded in myth. I didn't witness any of the events I'm about to relay, but it's a feel-good story for those of the lower ranks, simply because it demonstrates how the actions of a leader who cares can make a huge impact on morale.

At this juncture in the army, or at least at Fort Carson, the CIF issue and turn in process was a truly grueling affair. For the most part, when you sign for the gear, the ghouls employed at the CIF basically force the gear down your throat. You have to accept it "as is," whether or not it's actually clean or serviceable. The ghouls run you through the process so fast that you don't have time to check the gear for cleanliness or serviceability—not to mention that the largest portion of our army is manned by soldiers on their first (and probably only) duty assignment, so they really don't know what to look for while receiving their issue. When it comes to turning in your gear to the ghouls (who do this for a living), they scrutinize every piece of gear and know (by their extensive experience, as most have been in the employment of the CIF since Jesus Christ was the command sergeant major of the army) where to look for dirt or damage. These ghouls are all too happy to charge the soldier or kick the equipment back for a "redo." The soldier, having only ten days to clear, often just pays for the gear so he or she doesn't have to bother with the ass pain of dealing with the ghouls. Sometime in the past (I think Jesus was only a corporal then), businesses off post capitalized on this process and began the "field-gear cleaning" service, which can only lead to bad things.

Sometime in summer of 1995 at Fort Carson, Colorado, there was a rumor running around that if you wanted to get your field gear turned in at the CIF, all you needed to do was to take it down to a certain cleaners off post to have it cleaned. You'd have to bring your cleaned gear and the receipt to the CIF, and you could fly through the turn-in process. The workers didn't even check the gear; they just accepted it as clean and signed your paperwork.

The CG of the post got wind of this situation and decided to see for himself whether it was really a problem. He had his personal clerk draft him orders assigning him to the unit as a sergeant (SGT), and he donned a blouse with SGT stripes sewn on. He then went to the CIF with all the proper credentials and paperwork and was issued all the field gear required of an infantryman. Then he went out to his car and put the gear in the trunk.

Several days later he went back to the CIF and attempted to turn in this same gear. Because he didn't have the receipt from that particular cleaners, his gear was rejected, even though it hadn't been anywhere except the trunk of his car. He quietly recovered his gear, went back to his car, donned his proper blouse, and returned to the CIF, where he asked to see the management. "You're busted," he told them.

From what I understand, from that point forward, the CIF cleaned all of the soldiers' gear when the soldiers were to clear post. All a soldier had to do was take his or her equipment to the CIF and account for it all. As long as it was accounted for, it didn't have to be cleaned. Someone at CIF footed the bill, I reckon.

Shortly after I messed around with the IG and left my wake of destruction at Fort Carson, I returned home to Glen Rose, Texas, and moved in with my parents. The original plan was for my family and me to move into an old farmhouse that had resided on family land for close to eighty years. By now my wife and I had spawned a couple of kids, a boy and a girl. A friend of the family was living in the farmhouse, so we had to move in with my mom and dad for a few months until everything sorted itself out.

PART TWO
COMMISSION

PROFESSOR WHO?

BEFORE I STARTED COLLEGE IN JANUARY 1996, I HAD NO INTENTIONS OF joining the army again. My past experiences with not-so-good leaders and how they use their positions of authority to ride roughshod over their subordinates didn't set too well with me. I went to work for a contractor as a go-fer. When I first joined the army, the minimum wage was around four dollars an hour, and my father's contractor buddy offered me seven dollars an hour. At first I thought, *Wow, that's almost twice what I was making before I joined the army!!!* Only after I pulled down my first paycheck did I realize how well the army did pay.

I decided I needed an education to go along with my technical skills, not to mention that I had the Montgomery GI Bill available to me (at a whopping $473 a month), which was about half what I was making working as a go-fer, and all I had to do was sit through some classes for about twelve hours a week. That didn't sound too bad. Therefore I applied to a college close to my home.

I was accepted without too much fuss. I had to go through freshman orientation and a few other little odds and ends. One of the speakers at the orientation was a professor of military science (also known as a "PMS," not the more commonly known use of the acronym, but PMSs often have their moments), and his introduction speech intrigued me. He stood in front of all these freshmen while wearing his class As and said, "Any of y'all interested in joining ROTC (Reserve Officers Training Corps)?" He waited for a minute or two for a response then said, "All right, to hell with y'all then!" Then he exited the stage and went about his daily business. I thought, *I could work for a guy like that.* That afternoon I went to his office to introduce myself.

We were chatting about the program at that particular school, and I was surprised to find out that most of the cadets attending that university were prior-service military. Most had at least one tour of duty under their belts, and a couple of them were Desert Storm vets. He began to discuss the program in a little more detail when I noticed a coffee mug on his shelf, a New Mexico State University (NMSU) mug with the familiar Aggie logo. I remembered seeing a ton of those mugs in my youth, as my father had been the PMS at NMSU in the mid-1980s. I then asked him when he had graduated from NMSU.

His reply was, "Nineteen eighty-four."

I said, "Well, hell. That's when my father was the PMS there."

"Your father was LTC Jones?" he asked.

I gave him a resounding, "Hell, yeah!"

That was pretty much all she wrote; I was hooked from that point on. It turned out that the PMS had been one of my father's protégés, so I figured why not go with fate? I signed up, and the rest is written down in the following pages. There were a few knuckleheads I ran into along the way while attending college. One of them was the NCOIC of the program. Here's his story.

THE FIRE

THE YEAR BEFORE I SIGNED UP FOR THE PROGRAM, THERE WAS A LITTLE incident with this particular NCOIC and his tendency for pyromania. I need to give a little background regarding the school as well as ROTCisms before I continue with this story. This particular college was located in Central Texas. The school has a long tradition of producing cadets for the military that stretches back to before World War I. Several alumni had fought in the Spanish-American War, if not alongside Teddy Roosevelt, then somewhere near him. The school was located about an hour's drive north from Fort Hood and about an hour's drive east of Camp Bowie, a little-known national guard post. At one point, if I remember my history correctly, Camp Bowie was the largest military post in Texas, and right behind it was Fort Hood (then called "Camp Hood"). After World War II, there was a heated debate regarding which one would be kept as an active post and which would be put out to pasture. Obviously Fort Hood won out, as it's now the largest fort in Texas (and the free world). Camp Bowie never went away, however, and became a National Guard post. This post was open to ROTC units to conduct training exercises. Most ROTC detachments took advantage of every opportunity to train their cadets, and my school was no different. We trained there at least twice a semester on weekends when the National Guard wasn't using it.

At my college there were two "spirit" organizations that the ROTC detachment supported. One was a drill-and-ceremony team, and the other was a Ranger Challenge team. The ROTC Ranger Challenge team, not to be confused with the active-duty Ranger Challenge, was a motley crew of ragtag individuals. The team mostly consisted of a bunch of freshmen and sophomores (MS (Military Science) Is and IIs), a couple of juniors (MS IIIs), and one or two seniors (MS IVs). Their idea of "hard" was a joke to those of us who had been on active duty, but compared to the lame drill-and-ceremony team, there wasn't much of a choice. One had to join one or the other.

At these ROTC field exercises, generally speaking, the MS IIIs are the target audience for the training. The MS IVs are the graders and observer controllers, also known as OCs. They observe what's happening and control the situation so it doesn't get out of hand. They also grade the MS IIIs on their performance in a teacher-mentor role. Most of the lower classmen acted as the troops the MS IIIs led around, except for the Ranger Challenge team members. These Ranger Challenge members were used as opposing forces (OPFOR) during these training exercises. The NCOIC of the detachment was generally in charge of placing the OPFOR for these exercises.

On one particular field-training exercise, the NCOIC had dropped off most of the ROTC cadets at their start point. Then he took the OPFOR to their positions and gave them their instructions. He kept one of the lower classmen in the vehicle with him, as he intended to set up a bivouac site a little farther down the road on top of a hill. When he arrived at the bivouac site, he and the cadet set up the site. What this usually entails is setting out the rucksacks and other supplies, such as food, water, and propane heaters, so when the other cadets arrive they can top off their canteens and grab a bite of chow, as walking in the Texas heat all day tends to take a lot out of an individual. For some reason this time the NCOIC decided he wanted a fire.

This was his first knucklehead decision, as that year Texas was in the midst of one of the worst droughts in recent history and hadn't had a lick of rain for at least eight months. Everything was as dry as a tinderbox. The NCOIC dug a hole for a pit, threw some sticks into it, and then lit the sticks. Of course the sticks took to fire like gasoline. In no time he had a raging fire with glowing coals in his pit. The cadet and the NCOIC had lined the rucksacks in a military fashion, which means "dress right dress," with all the packs in a row, about twenty-five feet from the fire. Around the time the bivouac site was set up, the other cadets had reached their first objective and were in the midst of "contact" with the Ranger Challenge team. The NCOIC had been monitoring the cadets' movement on his handheld radio. He decided to go and have a look-see at what was going on. He told the cadet he had with him to stay at the bivouac site and watch the fire. Then he jumped into his large van and headed toward the objective to watch the action.

Just as the NCOIC was about halfway to the objective, the lonely cadet decided it was time for him to relieve himself and, being a good cadet and understanding proper field sanitation, took a stroll about a hundred yards from the bivouac site so he could handle his business. I'll bet he wasn't fifty yards from the bivouac site when he began to smell burning timbers. He finished his business and turned around to see an inferno of trees, leaves, rucksacks, and (oh, yes) boxes of propane cans. In a state of panic, he called to the NCOIC on the handheld radio and yelled, "Everything's on fire!"

The NCOIC must have halted in his tracks. I imagine his first thought was, *That can't be what he said.* He must have looked in his rearview mirror and seen a pillar of smoke. He then turned the van around and raced up the hill to find the lonely cadet with his BDU blouse off, beating the fire back as best as he could, which if you can imagine, was a losing battle. Around the time the NCOIC arrived at the site, the first of the propane canisters exploded. He quickly snatched up the cadet and hightailed it out of there.

He tore down the hill to the first objective and collected the other cadets. By this time the Range Control must have seen the smoke from the fire and called for help. All in all, about 750 acres of this national guard post burned, as well as all the equipment that was left on the hill.

Now, as to the equipment left on the hill, that is a point of contention. Around the time this field-training exercise was taking place, the PMS was conducting a 100-percent inventory of the NCOIC's supplies. He had discovered he was short a few things, roughly $150,000 worth of things. Before the field problem, the PMS was at a loss as to what he was going to do about the missing equipment, as usually the hand receipt holder (the PMS) is financially responsible for the loss. After the fire— well, let's just say all the shortages were accounted for in that fire.

THE COFFEE CUP

WHILE I WAS CONTRACTED WITH THE ROTC, I ALSO HAD REENLISTED WITH the guard. Seven of us cadets had decided to "double dip" and collect both a stipend from the active army as well as a National Guard paycheck. It wasn't really double dipping, as the funds came from two different sources, but it did mean more money in our pockets. Truthfully the money was pretty good, and we didn't have to do that much to earn it.

Most of the time, we could make it to our scheduled guard drill. From time to time, however, an ROTC outing conflicted with a guard drill, and we'd have to make up the time somehow. The NCOIC of the guard hall was a prick, one of types who thought, *So you want to abandon the NCO corps and become an officer, huh? I'll show you!* This prick took the opportunity to screw us over as often as he could. One particular weekend, three of us had missed drill due to class conflicts, and we had to make up the time.

One way we could make up our time was to coordinate with this prick and show up at the guard hall and act like slaves all day. He'd have us clean the armory, scrub the latrines, paint the woodshed—just about anything that needed doing. He always scrutinized every detail and told us how NCOs could do it better. What an asshole.

One weekend we were tasked with sweeping and mopping the entire armory floor, about an acre of concrete, as well as cleaning the NCOIC's office. While we were cleaning his office, he had to run to the store to grab some stuff and left us alone. One of my buddies took the opportunity to "brand" a couple of the NCOIC's things in his office. He took the NCOIC's coffee cup and rubbed the head of his pecker all around the inside of the rim. Next he grabbed a handful of pens and rubbed them all over his ass. Finally he took the phone receiver and rubbed it in the crack of his ass (I think he actually got part of the phone in his asshole— ewww).

When the NCOIC returned from his trip to the store, we asked if we could be released for lunch. He barked, "Make sure you're back at thirteen hundred hours!" As we walked out of the office, I heard the phone ring—ewww.

When we returned from lunch, he had a whole different attitude. At first he was mad as hell because while we gone to lunch the phone had rung and when he had answered it he smelled something awful on the receiver. He had us stand in front of him, and he was glaring at us. In his right hand he held his coffee cup and took a sip from it. My buddy then asked him, "Hey, how does my pecker taste?" The NCOIC's eyes went wide; he tossed the cup, bent over, and puked. Then he released us for the rest of the day. From that day forward, he never spoke to us again. And every time he walked by us, he turned a little green.

THE MAN WHO LOVED HIS NAME

WITH THIS NEXT STORY, I'M GOING TO HAVE TO TAKE A BREAK FROM LEAV-
ing names out of this book. We had this "older than dirt" cadet who was
thirty-two or thirty-three at the time, and the maximum age for a commission in that era was thirty-five, with prior service. This old cadet had
plenty of prior service. In fact we used to kid him, as he was probably the
only person I knew who'd had service in all three branches—the army,
the navy, and the air force. He had attended West Point as a cadet for
two years prior to joining the navy where he served on active duty for a
four year tour. Following his ETS from the navy he joined the air force
reserves while he attended college in order to complete his first bacca-
laureate degree. With his degree completed he joined the army National
Guard while he finished his first master's degree. When I met him, he was
working on his second master's degree and had decided to join up with
the ROTC detachment. Overall I think he had close to fourteen years
of service prior to ROTC. He was a studious-looking man, with glasses,
dark thinning hair, and a small build. He looked like the bad guy in *The
Princess Bride*, the "inconceivable" guy. His name was Dillard Coleman
Rape.

Dillard loved his last name. He didn't try to mask it or pronounce
it differently—just Rape. He used to joke about naming his first two
daughters "Statutory" and "Date." Once, during our senior year, some
women were picketing near the college library, chanting, "Rape is a
crime! Rape is a crime!" Dillard was right there in the middle of them,
yelling at the top of his lungs, "I am not a crime! I am a human being!"
I'm not sure if anyone other than me got the joke that day.

Another time, while we were still juniors, we were being graded on
the two-mile run (part of the army physical fitness test), and Dillard was
the last person in to be graded. He was almost always last because at his

age all he had to do was take the test, and as long as his heart was still beating, he passed it. Well, anyway, he was last and chugging along at his normal pace. An MS IV female, who thought she was rather hard-core, was grading him, and she was at the finish line, yelling at the top of her lungs, "Rape! Come on, Rape!" As she was yelling, some campus police drove up and asked her why she was yelling "Rape." She pointed down the lane and said, "His name is Rape." But when she pointed, there was no one there. You see, Dillard, seeing the campus police, had jumped into some bushes in order to hide. You gotta love a guy with that kind of sense of humor.

There was another time when his last name almost got some of us into more trouble than we could handle. There was a tradition at the ROTC detachment of having a formal at the end of the year. At this formal we'd all dress up and eat a "proper" meal; this was done in an effort to teach us heathens how proper folks dined. After the formal portion, in true college form, there was generally an after-formal keg party at one of the cadet's houses near the campus. At this party there was usually some heavy drinking, and from time to time some of the lightweight cadets would pass out. When one of the lightweights passed out, he or she was generally put into a bed in another room so the heavyweights could continue to party.

There was a young lady, not too unattractive, who attended this particular party on this particular night. She and another cadet, the one who rented the apartment, began to fool around a little, so they moved to one of the back rooms for more privacy. While in the back room, the young lady passed out, so the guy, being an honorable man, decided to let her sleep and went back to the main party room. In the morning this female cadet was supposed to meet her father, a LTC in the National Guard, for breakfast. She was late and didn't want to tell her father why she was late, so she concocted a date-rape story and accused the guy she had been fooling around with of drugging her drink so he could take advantage of her. This of course isn't what happened.

This LTC, after hearing his daughter's story, contacted the PMS and tried to apply some pressure so this wayward cadet would be punished. If I know anything about the PMS, his general feeling was one of, "If you can prove wrongdoing, then I'll take action. If not, then kiss off." Well, this male cadet was in a world of hurt. At this point he had little to go on except his story that he had done the honorable thing and let the young sleep in the room unmolested. The LTC began to apply a lot of pressure, not only on the PMS but also on the school. The male cadet, with little or no money, couldn't afford a lawyer to defend himself.

This is where the story takes a big turn. At that time most of us cadets were involved in what's known as the simultaneous membership program with the local National Guard unit, a program that was established so cadets could be members of the National Guard and the ROTC and draw a paycheck from both. The ROTC basically loaned its cadets to the National Guard for a weekend, and the cadets would gain some leadership experience to boot. The cadets would be placed in positions as "third LTs" (a nonexistent rank, but it's the best way to describe it). The commander of our local National Guard had been a lawyer and, early in his career, had won a civil-action lawsuit for which his cut was somewhere near $14 million. This commander still kept up with the law and practiced exclusively for guardsmen on a pro bono basis to handle little incidentals that cropped up. Typically these incidentals didn't include date-rape charges, but after this male cadet talked with him, he agreed to look into the case and see what he could do.

The lawyer went to work on the issue. A couple of my friends had been at the party while this "date rape" was supposed to have happened. My friend Dillard Rape was there. The lawyer asked each cadet who'd been at the party to write a sworn statement as to what he remembered. As all of them wanted to participate with proving our buddy innocent, they all agreed to help out. In the army we get used to calling one another by our last names, as they're printed on our uniforms and it's easier to remember who's who. So everyone called Dillard "Rape." As the cadets wrote down their sworn statements, they read something like this.

"Me, Rape, and so-and-so went to the party at so-and-so's apartment at such and such time. While there, me, Rape, and so-and-so saw such and such. Then me, Rape, and so-and-so did this or that."

After each cadet had written his statement, the lawyer, being a little brighter than most, asked everyone to write their statements again, but this time they needed to use first names rather than surnames.

APFT AT ADVANCED CAMP

A QUICK NOTE—THE FOREST IN WASHINGTON HAS TO BE ONE OF THE most beautiful places on earth. I've spent most of my life in Texas, and I'm used to the foliage and wildlife there. I'd never before seen a fern growing wild. Also there were these ants that lived in this "rain forest." They build their ant dens above ground, and some of these mounds grow to be four to six feet tall. These ants were endangered as well. We weren't supposed to hide behind the mounds for cover, and we were told to avoid them at all costs.

Every ROTC cadet, or so I'm told, has to go through advanced camp. When I went through ROTC, advanced camp was located at Fort Lewis, Washington, near the base of Mount Rainier, a spectacular sight. The fort itself is beautiful and alive with wilderness and wildlife. The year I went probably wasn't much different than any other year.

There are several problems with advanced camp, including the means by which cadets are evaluated. One of the first obstacles is the army physical fitness test (APFT), in which a cadet must do as many pushups and sit-ups as possible in two minutes (independently) then run two miles as fast as he or she can. The older one gets, the more time he or she has to pass it. For most cadets the time is around sixteen to seventeen minutes. In someone's infinite wisdom, it was decided to use the just commissioned LTs to grade the cadets. Most of these new LTs carry a little chip on their shoulder and look for anything to disqualify one of the repetitions performed (a pushup or sit-up). The bottom line was that you had to pass.

For my age group, I had to perform at least forty pushups and at least fifty sit-ups. I routinely maxed both during non-asshole-conducted APFTs (seventy-two push-ups and eighty-two sit-ups). So as a former enlisted cadet, I wasn't going to let one of these newly commissioned pecker heads take control of my destiny. When it was my turn, I climbed into the proper pushup position and looked the grader right in the eye. I then exaggerated each movement, making sure he counted every repetition. I mean, after all, all I needed was forty, right? When I got to forty, I quickly knocked out ten more, got up, and walked to the back of the line.

Wouldn't you know it—the LT said, "Hey, you still have thirty seconds left."

"I passed. You counted fifty," I replied.

He returned, "You got up early. You're disqualified." (This wasn't in the regulations or in the APFT manual.)

Instead of arguing I shrugged and said, "If you say so."

I did the same for the sit-ups, and the conversation went about the same. I currently had two "disqualifications." But I had a plan. You see, while you're doing the events, they have another cadet next to you, and this was my witness. After the two-mile run, I approached the head officer in charge and told him what had happened. He proceeded to educate the young LT, whose only come back was, "I was just trying to motivate him." Silly LTs.

THE STX LANES

A COUPLE OF WEEKS LATER, MY SQUAD (ABOUT TWELVE CADETS—TEN guys and two gals) were doing situational training exercises, also known as "STX lanes." In these exercises we received briefings regarding what we were supposed to do and then an evaluation of what we did. We did this out in the field, walking through the forest, avoiding the ant mounds. Between lanes (we did anywhere from six to eight a day), we did what was called a "patrol base." This is where everyone lies down in a large circle, with the leaders in the middle planning the next lane.

I was chosen as a team leader. The squad leader, who sat in the middle, called the team leaders in and issued his orders. We team leaders (two of us) then went back to our teams and explained the plan. While I was briefing my team (five cadets—four guys and one gal), one of the guy's faces turned white as ash. I asked him what was wrong. He looked like he was about to faint.

He grabbed his groin area, quickly unbuckled his belt, and pulled his pants down around his ankles. He then grabbed his pecker, and as hard as I tried not to, I had to look. Hanging off the head of his pecker was one of those "endangered" ants. He, rather gently, picked the ant off his pecker, flung it away, then passed out cold.

It took us a few moments to stop laughing before we took the time to check to see if he was OK. We splashed some water on his face (after pulling his pants up first) and let him sit for a little while. Soon the color returned to his face, and he said he was ready to go. I finished my brief, and then we grabbed our equipment and headed off to the next encounter along the lanes.

We'd been moving along at a fair clip when I (being the front team leader) spied "movement" on our objective. I stopped and put up the signal for "eyes on" and "movement ahead." Then I gave the hand and arm signals for my team to begin to disperse. I noticed that the same fella who'd had the incident with the ant dropped all his gear and took off running as he waved his hands all about his head. The tactical officer (TAC)[23] chased after him. I truly didn't know what to make of it, so I just continued to perform the team-leader duties.

After we had secured the position, the TAC returned, carrying most of the "runaway" cadet's gear. Apparently he had kicked a ground hornets' nest, and the hornets didn't take too kindly to the intrusion. When we saw the cadet again a few days later, he had golf-ball-size welts on his face and arms. Some guys don't have any luck.

The only real problem with Washington State is that it's a lot wetter and a whole lot colder than Texas. One night, as we were sleeping in a bivouac site, I had my poncho and liner covering me. In Texas I wouldn't have needed the poncho liner, and I would have slept warmly. In Washington I was shivering like you wouldn't believe. When I awoke the next morning, there was ice on my poncho. Needless to say I was cold the entire summer. I swear, the low in Washington's summer is cooler than the low in Texas's winter. I was shivering all the way home on the airplane. When I finally arrived in Texas and walked outside, I felt the heat on my skin and thought, *I'm home*. I didn't let my wife turn the AC on in the car the entire way home. I needed time to thaw out.

The next year passed without much happening, and soon after, I was commissioned as a second lieutenant (more commonly known as a "2LT" or "butter bar," as the gold rank fades and looks like butter). The first stop for a new 2LT is Officer Basic Course (OBC). I was commissioned in the field artillery, and the OBC was located at Fort Sill, Oklahoma. So once again I packed up the family and moved—this time to Lawton, Oklahoma, just outside Fort Sill. We bought a house, and I reported for duty.

---

23. The TAC is basically any individual in charge and not a cadet during this training. Some are cool and some aren't. Some are tactical experts and some are finance experts. It just depends on the luck of the draw who you get to evaluate you.

THE TORNADO

THE MOST INTERESTING THING THAT HAPPENED WHILE I WAS IN OBC WAS the tornado. About halfway through the course, the other 2LTs and I were in the field calling for fire[24] on a stationary target. We were fumbling around, and some of the 2LTs were a little better than others, but by and by, we were figuring out what to do.

We were sitting on a set of metal bleachers in the middle of an open field. Early in the morning, the weather had been fine, but as is wont to happen in Oklahoma, the weather suddenly changed. The sky began to darken, and the wind picked up. Rumor had it that no tornado ever had touched down on the Fort Sill Indian reservation. From what I was told, that's the reason the Native Americans called it "Medicine Bluff."

I was sitting next to this citified fellow from New York or some other Yankee city who never had experienced what we in Texas call "severe weather." He asked me if a tornado was coming. I looked around and said, "Nah, just a little rain and maybe some hail." Then I added, "Don't worry. I'll let you know when a tornado is coming." That seemed to pacify him, as he went back to watch the other 2LTs bumble around with their calls for fire.

About twenty minutes later, the wind picked up; the sky turned a grayish green; and I swear the rain was coming in from two different directions simultaneously. I leaned over to the city fella and said, "I'd start worryin' if I were you." He then jumped up and ran for the nearest ditch, along with the other 2LTs and the instructor. Me? Well, I stayed

---

24. Calling for fire is the act of the forward observer (FO), who identifies a target, figures out where it is on a map, then sends the coordinates to a fire direction center (FDC). The FDC then computes the correct shell-fuse-powder combination for the gun crew to load. The gun crew loads the gun, pulls the lanyard, and—boom—if everything is done correctly, the target is destroyed. We call that "steel on target." Most 2LTs really suck at this, so we adjust on the target. To adjust, the FO sends in corrections, and the same process is followed until there's steel on target.

right there in the bleachers. My dad always had taught me to face your impending death by offering it the last act of defiance (a stiff middle finger). If I'm going to die, I'll die on my feet—or in this case, sitting in the bleachers. Lightning was flashing. Thunder was cracking. For those not used to this kind of weather, I suspect they thought the world was coming to an end. Me? I just watched for the funnel cloud.

Off in the distance, I saw the tail of a funnel cloud begin to form. Then I saw the funnel cloud descend toward the ground. It must have been fifty feet or so from touching down. Then it sucked back up and went about its merry way. For all I know, the legend that no tornado has touched Fort Sill is still untarnished.

MPS ARE SO MUCH FUN

ONE DAY, AS I WAS DRIVING HOME FROM WORK, AN MP PULLED UP BE-
hind me. His flashers were on, and I thought, *Oh, hell*. As LTs we
always had been told to watch out for MPs at Fort Sill, as they were
highly motivated to give us tickets. To give an LT a ticket was the
highlight of any young MP private's day. This is what ran through my
head that moment. I pulled my truck over and sat really still. I knew
I hadn't been speeding, and I hadn't run any stop signs or stoplights
(I was extremely careful). The MP walked up to the side of my truck,
knocked on the window, and said, "Sir, I need you to step out of the
vehicle." I reached over, opened the door, and stepped out, ready to
give this little MP a piece of my mind. Suddenly I was getting bear-
hugged! I didn't know what to think.

After the initial shock wore off, I recognized one of my oldest buddies
from high school. A quick note—the town where I grew up was rather small.
In fact it was so small it was prudent to marry a woman from out of town
just to be sure the two of you weren't related. So the fact that my mother
knew his mother shouldn't be a big shock to anyone. Apparently, my buddy
had been there about a year or so before I arrived. My mother, knowing my
buddy was assigned there mentioned to my buddy's mother that I was newly
assigned to Fort Sill. In turn, his mother mentioned to him I was there. All
these mentioning's about my present duty assigned must have slipped my
mother's mind as she never mentioned anything to me.

After he and I reminisced for a bit I invited him and his wife out to
my house for dinner. His wife was also originally from our home town
and as the high school we attended was as small as the town, we all knew
each other. It was nice to have friends in this new place.

Several months later I was assigned to a unit at Fort Sill. This was
fortunate, I might add, because I had bought a house in Lawton, Oklahoma
without knowing whether or not I was going to stay there. Had I been
moved elsewhere, I would have been screwed. I reported to my first unit,

which was a multiple launch rocket system (MLRS[25]) unit. When I arrived at my new unit, I met another LT who was about a year ahead of me. The first thing he said to me was, "Where are you from?" I replied, "Texas." He looked offended and said rather rudely, "Texas sucks." I looked him square in the eye and said, "Well, fuck you, too!" This seemed to get his attention. He said, "Well, not the state, the school." I had to agree with him as I am not much of a fan of UT Austin (commonly referred to at just "Texas" by a lot of folks in the military). But our relationship never really improved after that. You see, he was from Nebraska. The only things I know about Nebraska are that it's flat, they grow corn, and the Huskers are there. Apparently UT Austin had thrashed his beloved Huskers rather well the night before. I didn't even know they had played.

All I knew was this guy was an ass. So I took to needlin' him every chance I got ("to needle" is a Southern term that means to poke a person repeatedly—generally all in fun, but sometimes it comes to more). He had a Nebraska Cornhuskers license-plate frame on the front of his truck. I replaced it with a rainbow license-plate frame. I also bought a bunch of rainbow magnet stickers and put them on his vehicle about once a week.

I soon took to showing up earlier than this LT and started parking in his "assigned" parking spot. Needless to say, this ticked him off something fierce and led to a kind of cold war. Who could get there earlier? One night I just left my truck there overnight and had my wife pick me up. This infuriated the other LT. He parked his truck behind mine and told me he wouldn't move. I shrugged it off and called my MP buddy and informed him there was a truck double-parked behind mine. In no time a tow truck arrived and towed the LT's truck away. I waited until his truck was hooked up to the tow truck then walked inside and said, "Uh, your truck's being towed." He dropped everything and ran outside to chase the tow truck down the road.

---

25. The MLRS is arguably the most lethal weapon on the conventional battlefield. Each rocket in the system is designed to take out a five-hundred-meter-circumference area. Each rocket has 644 submunitions (little hand-grenade-like bomb-lets), each with about a fifteen-meter blast radius dispersed over the target in a five-hundred-meter circle. The shrapnel from the sub-munitions can penetrate up to twelve inches of reinforced concrete. The bottom line is this thing packs one hell of a punch. The army, at this time, used this weapons system to suppress enemy air defense, destroy enemy command posts or signal units, destroy fuelers, etc. They used to call it "the general's trump card," as the general would play it during a decisive moment of the battle in order to punch the enemy with overwhelming firepower.

STRANGE ASS KID

ONE OF THE PRIVATES IN MY BATTERY WHEN I FIRST SHOWED UP WAS, well, to put it euphemistically, one strange ass kid. He was about medium height with a slight build. He had brown hair, green eyes, and he wore glasses. When I first met him, he seemed smart enough. When given a job to do, he was rather efficient at accomplishing the mission without much supervision. These are not the things that make him strange. It was his extracurricular activities that will blow your mind.

As a side note, I first suspected something strange about him when he asked me if, since I was a lieutenant and all lieutenants outranked the first sergeant, if I—providing I had cause—could drop the first sergeant for push-ups. I thought about this question for a few minutes before I answered him. I was trying to figure out what his angle was; a few of the thoughts running through my head were: Why would a lieutenant have cause to drop a first sergeant? If a lieutenant tried, how many pieces of the lieutenant would they have to find before they could charge the first sergeant with murder?

I told the kid that, technically, yes, a lieutenant could drop a first sergeant, but, if he did there would be hell to pay–if not from the first sergeant himself, the battery commander would more than likely want to break a foot off in the lieutenant's ass. So, yes, he "could", but, no, he shouldn't. My answer seemed to satisfy the kid for a time.

Other than his strange question and a few other small oddities about this kid, nobody would have suspected anything out of the ordinary. Truthfully, when the police called the battery commander about this kid and his extracurricular activities it was out of the blue. Nobody could have foreseen what this kid was up to after hours or happened next.

Somewhere along the way this kid had gotten hold of an old police cruiser. Not too hard considering these cruisers are being sold at auction all the time. It was when he had it painted to match the current police vehicles, attached whoopee lights, bought a radar gun, and hooked up a siren, then proceeded to pull people over and issue citations that it became a problem. Where he got the citations from nobody really knew. It was thought there might have been some older citations left in the glove box of his cruiser but that is pure speculation. But, that isn't where this kid's problems stopped.

Apparently, after the police picked him up for illegally detaining drivers, someone had ordered a psyche evaluation and he failed it with impunity. This kid was nuttier than a fruitcake! The decision was made and approval given for him to be placed in pretrial confinement. As is protocol, an inventory of all his personal belongings is made and they are placed in boxes and stored in the supply room until his final disposition is made. When the NCOs opened his wall locker they discovered a set of officer class A's decked out with captain bars. Someone had the inkling to check out the security footage at the PX, commissary, and other installations on and off post. Low and behold, there was video footage of this kid parading around the PX on the training side of post, dropping privates (still in training) for push-ups.

I'm not sure what happened to him after he was placed in pretrial confinement. I suspect he was discharged and sent to a funny farm somewhere in hopes of treating his mental illness. I sure hope this kid wasn't serial-killer crazy. Or, if he is, I hope I'm not on his list...

FIRST RANGE

SOON AFTER MY ARRIVAL TO MY NEW UNIT I WAS GIVEN MY FIRST REAL task—a range to run. It was a .50 cal range, the weapon system known as the M2 or Ma Deuce and is one of the best weapons ever entered into the army inventory. It remains mostly unchanged even after over a hundred years of service. It serves as both an air defense weapons system and an effective ground unit weapon system. Anyway, I digress.

As this was my first range I was rather excited. I went through the proper channels and procedures for organizing and coordinating the necessary resources for my range, briefed the operations officer and the battalion commander on my plan, and got the green light to execute. The day of execution arrived; I took my platoon out to the range, set up and waited for folks to arrive so they could qualify on their Ma Deuces. Out at the range there is an observation tower, a set of bleachers, and an ammunition shack[26]. We set up a butcher block—a large display with instructions written on it to inform folks what was expected out at our range.

My platoon sergeant (the second in charge of a platoon) told me to sit in the HMMWV and watch the radio. I had been enlisted at one point so I knew a little bit about the army. I had never been a platoon leader before nor had I ever run a range before; and, I knew a lot of platoon sergeants were skeptical about former enlisted officers as we tend to want to "take over" and run the platoon. The running (or operations) of a platoon is the purview of the platoon sergeant. The overall management of the platoon rests on the lieutenant. So, he and I had talked about this in the past and I was content to let him run things—boy, would I be sorry.

About halfway through the day, while I was sitting in the HMMWV

---

26. The Ammo shack is a little 10x10 building designed for a crew of soldiers to occupy and keep the ammo under cover and out of the elements.

acting as an over paid radio operator, the lazy day was interrupted by a KKRACCKK!!! Quickly followed by a TWANG!!! I learned quickly these were the telltale sounds of a round impacting in the bleachers. Everything seemed to freeze in place.

I jumped out of the hummer and ran over to the bleachers in order to see if anyone was hurt. Fortunately, the bleachers were empty but sure as shit there was a hole (a rather large one) extremely visible right through the bleachers. I looked at my platoon sergeant wanting an explanation. He said, "Hell sir, I don't know what happened but, don't worry about it. I know the guys out at range control. We'll be able to cover this up no problem." I had my doubts. I was ultimately concerned about where the bullet ended up. More than likely it landed harmlessly in the field just behind the bleachers, however, a .50 bullet has a lot of inertia and can travel several miles if circumstances are ideal. I knew that there was at least the potential we had killed or injured someone miles away. Fortunately, I never heard back from range control about any incidents that day as a result of my wayward round.

At the end of the day I reported to the battalion commander about the results of my day's range; the number of folks who attended and number of folks who qualified. We had had a pretty successful day with about 30 systems running through the range (we had expected about 35) and all had qualified. I carefully avoided anything about the bleachers. When I finished reporting and answering all his questions, I saluted and said, "Sir, this concludes my report."

He returned my salute and I started for the door. Just before I reached it he asked, "Ray, do you have anything else to tell me?"

My heart almost stopped. My palms began to sweat. My throat went completely dry. I knew he knew what had happened. I turned around and held my head low to the ground.

"Yes sir, we had a round that somehow hit the bleachers."

"Ray, I'm glad you told me. If you had lied I was going to fire you," he calmly said. I did receive a thorough ass chewing but I didn't get fired. I had to file a report and do an investigation into the incident as punishment, but overall I learned a couple of life lessons about the incident. One, don't try to hide the truth; and two, my platoon sergeant was a piece of shit.

THE INTERNAL THIEF

SOON AFTER WE (THE BATTERY) WENT TO THE FIELD, I HAD A RECON SERgeant who drove for me and was supposed to "show me the ropes." When we went to the field out at Fort Chaffee, Arkansas, for a thirty-day field exercise, I'd brought along a bunch of my own equipment, as I'd been enlisted at one point and knew a thing or two about field survival. After we'd driven around and conducted several missions over a week or two, I started to notice that some of my equipment was missing. First it was just small items: a coffee mug, a compass, and other little things. Then later bigger things were missing, such as a CamelBak and a poncho liner. I could understand my leaving small stuff lying around; I didn't think I had, but I could see it happening. The larger items—now that was just downright unusual for me, so I began to suspect a bit of foul play and started to lock my stuff up rather tightly and did accountability anytime we moved.

Several months later, when we went to the field again and this particular sergeant was no longer my driver, I began to see my things appearing in other people's vehicles or hanging off their gear. I knew that stuff was mine, as those items had several unique marks on them. When I confronted these other individuals and asked where they'd gotten their nifty items, they all responded with "Sergeant So-and-So sold it to me out at Chaffee." Apparently this recon sergeant had rather sticky fingers and liked to sell things that weren't his. There was nothing I could do, however, as I didn't have my name on any of the items.

In the end, this same sergeant got what was coming to him. After he left my platoon, he began to beg to go to Korea. After he submitted several transfer requests, his wish was finally answered. As he was an NCO, he was authorized to clear post by himself with minimal supervision. All he really had to do was show up to PT in the morning in battle dress uniform (BDUs) and say, "I have such and such appointment today." A soldier normally gets ten working days to clear post and the unit, so he seemed to be doing everything by the book. He always had this little smirk on his face as he went about his business, and we all thought he was happy to be going to Korea. (I was happy just to get him out of the battery!)

When the day finally came for him to sign out of the unit on leave, he didn't show up to formation. One of the LTs went over to staff duty, the place where one signs out for leave, and found this NCO's name in the "signed out" column. We all figured that he was gone for at least a year and that none of us would have to deal with him anymore.

About three months later, one of the training-room clerks walked up to an LT buddy of mine and said, "Sir, you have to do something about Sergeant So-and-So. He's in my house making passes at my wife." Apparently this NCO signed out of the unit but never got on the plane to Korea! He had just been hanging out at this young soldier's house for three to four months, collecting a paycheck. Since Korea had such a high turnaround in regard to soldiers, it was possible the gaining unit never would have known he was inbound. The first sergeant sent a group of NCOs down to the young soldier's house to collect our wayward NCO (soon to be SPC) and put him under guarded escort. When we finished the Article 15 for AWOL, the first sergeant personally took the NCO to the airport and watched him get on the plane for Korea. Good things come to good people.

THE DUD PLATOON SERGEANT

THE FIRST PLATOON SERGEANT I HAD AS A PLATOON LEADER WAS A REAL winner. He was the type of PSG that could break even the best of platoon leaders. When I first arrived at the battery, I was sent to second PLT and informed that the PSG was also new. However, as I was prior enlisted and the PSG was a senior staff sergeant (SSG) with eighteen years of service, I thought everything should work out just fine. The first time I talked with the man, though, I got the feeling he was nothing more than a piece of shit. The fact that he was incompetent was especially clear after the range incident with the "wholy bleachers." He had a way of smirking at you while he was talking that made you think he wasn't quite sure if you knew he was incompetent.

Being that I was a prior-enlisted officer and had a little experience under my belt, I picked up on this rather quickly. I hadn't been a field artilleryman while I was enlisted; my only field artillery experience at this point had been in the officer basic course, so I didn't have much room to call bullshit on what he was telling me unless we were in the motor pool. I did call bullshit on him a few times, and his standard answer was, "I was just testing you." My ass.

There was this one time when we went to the field and we were supposed to be evaluated. I was rather nervous and wanted everything to be "perfect." I was supposed to conduct a recon of the proposed area of operation and since the roads in front of the battery headquarters always closed around 0600 because PT was being conducted in that area. "No traffic" meant "safe for running." So I told my PSG to have my HMMWV ready to leave on the recon by 0530. I walked out to where my vehicle was supposed to be at 0530, but there was no vehicle. I was rather ticked, as this was to be my first "graded" field problem, and things were already starting off badly. I found my PSG and asked him where my HMMWV was. He told me he had passed the message along to my driver but didn't know where it was. I scrambled around looking for the vehicle when I ran into my driver.

I asked him what he knew, and he said that he had no clue where the HMMWV was and that the PSG hadn't told him anything about it (this driver was the same winner from previous story). I finally tracked down my HMMWV in the motor pool. The launcher chiefs were using it for shuttling men and equipment back and forth from the battery to the motor pool and told me the PSG hadn't told them anything about my recon. Now I was getting rather suspicious, so I confronted my PSG, who chalked the problem up to "miscommunication."

I knew something was wrong, but I had nothing but gut instinct telling me so. When we finally got to the field, I remember him almost cutting half his finger off when the heater hose fell off on his side of the HMMWV. For some stupid reason, he put his finger in the hole. Well, duh—there's a fan down there! What do you think pushes the hot air out? We had to medevac him back to garrison for that, and I ended up not having a PSG for the rest of the field problem.

ALMOST A
COMPLETE FAILURE

WE CHUGGED ALONG FOR ROUGHLY SIX MORE MONTHS WHEN WE FINALLY
were deployed to Fort Chaffee, Arkansas, for an ARTEP[27]. I'd have to say
this was one of the worst field problems I've ever experienced. It rained
for about three weeks straight. If you've never been to Fort Chaffee, Arkansas, let me explain.

I have a theory. I believe the army, back in the day, decided where to
put forts and posts by sending out a man on a horse and running that
horse as far as it could run, and when the horse died from exhaustion,
they'd go twenty more miles and set up a post. In the case of Fort Chaffee,
it was a swamp—before the rain hit. After one night of rather hard rain,
the swamp was a lake. I remember parking my command post on a hill
in a tree line. The next morning, after a night's hard rain, I could have
fished off the front of it.

We arrived at Fort Chaffee and began what the army calls "building
combat power." In an MLRS platoon, at this juncture in history, I had
three launchers, one command post, and two HMMWVs. In the field
I had anywhere from two to six HEMTT (Heavy Expanded Mobility
Tactical Truck) ammunition trucks[28] with trailers that could haul a

---

27. An ARTEP is a field-training exercise where you get graded. The ARTEP is generally
where the battery/battalion commanders are either rated as really good—or really bad.
Basically ARTEPs are career makers or breakers.

28. HEMTTs are pronounced as "Hemmets." The trailers are called HEMATs which
stands for Heavy Expanded Mobility Ammunition Trailer. In an MLRS unit the ammo
is large. The rockets come in six packs (six rockets per pod) and missiles are one to a
pod. The pods are about 3 ft x 3 ft x 12 ft. Each HEMTT can carry four pods and each
trailer can carry an additional four pods for a total of eight pods or 48 rockets. As stated
earlier, each rocket can destroy up to a 500 meter radius area. Multiply that by 48 and
you have a 24.000 meter radius (24 kilometers) destroyed. What a wonderful system…

bunch of ammunition around. We went out into the "box" to begin training. Within twenty-four hours, all my launchers were broken; my HMMWV was broken; and the only thing I had operational was the PSG's HMMWV and the command post. The launchers were still able to drive around; the battery commander wanted me to get some training out of the exercise, so I was to "pretend" my launchers were operational and still conduct missions, which I did. Eventually we fixed most of the maintenance problems, but this was an indication that maintenance wasn't being conducted to standard. As I'd been a mechanic, I found this unacceptable. I had trusted my PSG to do the right thing, and he had failed me.

Speaking of the PSG, he was nowhere to be found. All this time I kept wondering where my PSG was and what he was doing. The job of a PSG in the field is rather easy. He or she is in charge of "beans, bullets, and Band-Aids," meaning food, ammunition, and the medics. There are a few other little details, but if a PSG gets those three down, almost everything else will take care of itself.

After about a week in the field, we had a live fire scheduled for the battery. The night before the live fire, there was a battery meeting, and all the leaders were supposed to be there to discuss the ins and outs of the live fire. You see, a live fire for MLRS PLTs is an exciting time, as they only get to do them about twice a year. The rockets are rather expensive, and we wanted to take advantage of the situation. As I pulled into the battery operations area (BOC), my PSG was nowhere in sight. The battery commander (BC) asked me if the PSG knew about the meeting, and I replied, "Yes, I passed the information off to him via FM [radio] earlier in the day." We waited for about fifteen minutes, and the BC said, "To hell with it. You'll have to brief your PSG as soon as you find him." About this time we heard some traffic on the battery net. I remember hearing my PSG calling to ask the location of the BOC.

Then another call came over the battalion net. "Deep Strike Six [my BC], this is Proud Rocket Six [the battalion commander (CMR)]. One of your HMMWVs has just T-boned my HMMWV." As all the other HMMWVs within the battery were accounted for outside the BOC, except my PSG's, it didn't take a rocket scientist to figure out which HMMWV had run into the BN CMR, but the BC had to ask. "PR Six, this is DS Six. Which HMMWV was it?" To which the reply was, "DS Twenty-Nine." My PSG.

After the accident was cleaned up, we found that no one was hurt (just my pride), and there was no serious vehicle damage. This accident, however, spurred a lot of questions within the leadership of my battery, especially since the location of the accident wasn't anywhere near the BOC area.

Q1: "What the hell was he doing over there?"
A1: "The PL didn't tell me where to go." Of course the PSG claimed I had given him the wrong data (all *good* PSGs blame the LT).

Q2: "Who was driving?"
A2: "The PSG."

Q3: "Where was his driver?"
A3: "He was asleep in the passenger seat."

Q4: "Why was he driving without his headlights on?"
A4: "The PSG was using his night-vision goggles without the head harness." (He was holding them in his left hand.)

Q5: "If he had the radio receiver in one hand and the NVGs in the other, what was he holding onto the steering wheel with?"
A5: (The silence was thunderous.)

The PSG was in tears. He had a breakdown and was sobbing to the first sergeant about how all the launcher chiefs were against him and how the platoon leader wasn't giving him the correct data. I confronted the BC and asked what I was supposed to do with a man like that. His reply was that I should confront him and tell him that the whole world wanted his head on a platter and that I was the only one who wanted to keep him. See, in the BC's eyes, if I were to do this one act, it would cement a relationship between the PSG and me, and we'd emerge as a solid team. I thought, *I don't think I want to forge a solid relationship with this sort of guy.* But I did as all LTs are supposed to do and said, "Yes, sir." Then I did exactly as I was instructed to do. I even used very similar words to what he suggested.

The next morning was the live fire. We were briefed regarding the plan, and we all left to conduct our portion of the planning process and to brief our lower echelons. This happened without incident. My plan called for the platoon to gather near the live-fire area early in the morning. I met my launchers at the rendezvous site. I had my command post there, and the ammo trucks were there, but my PSG was nowhere to be found. I tried raising him on the radio to no avail. I waited for fifteen to twenty minutes then called him on the platoon net. No answer. I was rather ticked, so I led my platoon away from that site without the PSG. I occupied the new site, set security out, and waited until the sun rose. I halfway figured the PSG would show up sometime during the early morning, but he didn't.

This created a serious problem for my platoon and me, as we were supposed to be the first ones to shoot at first light. The SOP for the battery was a two-man check on the launchers before they shot. I (the PL) would "safe" the platoon, and the PSG would "safe" the PL. Simple— except impossible without a PSG. The first sergeant kept asking me, "Where's your messed-up PSG?" The time to fire came and went. The other platoon went out to shoot in order to give me more time to find my PSG, but I couldn't find him. After the other PLT shot, we waited for a few minutes when the first sergeant suggested that the PSG from the other PLT "safe" my PLT for me. I had no room for argument. After the shoot was over and my launchers had cleared the firing point, my PSG rolled up to the area.

The first sergeant went off like a Roman candle. Before I could take one step in that direction, he was digging all up in the PSG's ass. I wanted to crawl away and not hear what was happening. The end result was that I got a new PSG. As to what had happened? Well, the PSG's story was that he ran out of fuel. This is a most fundamental no-no in the army, as the fuel is free. Even the lowest private knows you're supposed to top off your vehicle every chance you get. In most battalions, to run out of fuel was an automatic field-grade Article 15[29]. In this case it was reason for cause and removal from the unit. The next PSG I got was a dream, so I reckon good things can happen.

---

29. An Article 15 is a non-judicial punishment in which the individual can be stripped of at least one stripe, loses a half month's pay for up to two months, and can have extra duty for up to forty-five days. There are two types of Article 15s. One is a Company (or Battery) grade and the other is a Field Grade. The difference is the amount of punishment being dealt out as well as the rank of the officer (either company grade or field grade) signing the paperwork. A Company grade officer is 2nd Lieutenant, 1st Lieutenant, or a Captain; and a Field grade officer is a Major, Lieutenant Colonel, or a Colonel.

THE DREAM PLATOON SERGEANT

SOON AFTER I RECEIVED MY NEW PSG, THE ATTITUDE AND DIRECTION MY platoon took was 180 degrees from where it had been. The section chiefs (MLRS speak for the guys who commanded and controlled the launchers) were thrilled. The only flaw I saw in my new PSG was his fondness for the word "motherfucker." I swear, he couldn't get a sentence out without at least two "motherfuckers" accounted for.

As soon as we returned from the field, we went through what's called "recovery." This is when soldiers clean and service all their gear and prepare it for the next field exercise. The soldiers do most of the work, while the PL supervises. My wife had brought the kids by, as I wanted them to get a chance to crawl around on the launchers, and I wanted to introduce my wife to my new PSG, the one who had saved my platoon.

The new PSG had one other slight flaw. He couldn't seem to remember anyone's name, so he made up names for everyone. I was "motherfucking PL," which seemed natural. The first section chief was "motherfucking first section." You get the idea. The PSG's driver—God bless him—had a lazy eye, so naturally he was "motherfucking one-eyed Jack." The first time I was about to introduce my wife to this great platoon sergeant, he was looking for his driver and said, "Hey, motherfucking PL, have you seen motherfucking one-eyed Jack?"

My wife was rather shocked, but the PSG didn't miss a beat. He stuck out his hand and said, "'Morning, ma'am."

Life in that battery was good to great from that time on[30]. We

---

30 Artillery units are called "batteries"; this, or so I'm told, goes back to our ancient heritage when the artillery was once part of the engineer corps, and they used battering rams to batter down the doors of a castle or keep. Later, when the first howitzers were used for the same purpose, they were called batteries. So the name stuck.

eventually won the post "best platoon" competition and did all the great tasks that benevolent title bestowed—things like doing live fire shoots for VIPs (very important pricks), driving vehicles in parades, etc.

NOT IN MY FOOD CHAIN!

AS SOON AS WE RETURNED TO FORT SILL AND COMPLETED OUR RECOVERY, things settled back to "normal," at least for a little while. About a month or so later, the battalion wanted us to head back out to the field for another artillery live fire. Somehow the battalion had gotten its hands on a shitload of rockets, and one thing you should know about artillerists is that they love to shoot.

We had just returned from a battalion-qualifying exercise, and everyone was "qualified," so this live fire was supposed to be a walk in the park. In the meantime, the battalion had picked up a new battalion executive officer (XO), and we had picked up a new battery commander. The new battalion XO was somewhat of a cocky, I-know-more-than-you, West Point graduate prick. He had grown up in a cannon-artillery world rather than a rocket-launcher-artillery world. There are some similarities, but there are more differences than one would like to admit. The XO had the habit of sticking his nose in areas we thought were operating just fine, finding what he thought were issues, and telling us how to fix these issues when there weren't any real issues. Sound confusing? Here's an example.

We were setting up our fire direction center (FDC) in order to rehearse the upcoming live fire, and the XO decided he wanted to observe the young LTs in action. We had everything set up in accordance with our SOP and were computing safety data for the live fire[31]. We were having some issues connecting with the launcher digitally, and the way the MLRS system is put together, one has to talk digitally to the launcher in order to compute safety. This is one significant difference between

---

31. Safety is paramount for an artilleryman. You don't want to drop rounds on the good guys, so you have to predict where the rounds will land. We do this by computing safety, where we take all the "knowns;" add a little bit to the left and the right, farther and closer; then draw a box around it and call that "safety." Truthfully it's a relatively scientific computation that took me six weeks in OBC to understand, and it works.

the two worlds of cannons and rockets. In the cannon-artillery world, you don't need the cannon to predict the ballistics of the round; you use a tabular firing table (TFT)[32] and charts and darts[33]. The XO, not really understanding how the MLRS system operates, got really upset. He started hollering at us, calling us lazy artilleryman for not setting up our charts and darts—accusing us of not understanding how artillery works, and just generally making a complete ass out of himself. He did this in the most unprofessional manner and right in front or our enlisted soldiers.

The NCOs, rightfully so, told the enlisted soldiers to take a break, and they exited the FDC, so the younger guys were protected from his idiocy. After the soldiers left the tent, the real hollering began. I, being the boldest of the LTs, asked the XO how much he knew about launchers. He looked at me as if I had a pecker growing out of my forehead. He squared up to me and said, "I've been an artilleryman for close to twenty years. I've forgotten more about this stuff than you'll ever know."

I replied, "Apparently not. We don't have charts and darts on our hand receipts. They've never existed in a launcher property book. We don't use them. This is the only way to compute data."

One of the other LTs reached for the manual to show the XO we weren't just lazy, stupid LTs, and when he handed it to the XO, the XO got really mad and threw the book at the LT. He then said, "You'll go get the charts and darts. And you'll set them up." I looked him square in the eye and said, "No, we won't. You are nowhere in my food chain. You're interrupting our training event with your ignorance. Leave."

At this point there were only really two courses of action the XO could take—one, start a fight; or two, walk away. Fortunately he decided to walk away. As he did so, he said, "You can't kick me out of your training event. I'm the XO!" I replied, "I just did."

A few minutes later, I began to feel rather remorseful about the whole episode. I walked outside and told the NCO to continue troubleshooting the connectivity issue, as I was going for a walk to cool off. As I walked away, I pulled out my cell phone and called my new battery commander.

---

32. The TFT is also known as the "Big Brown Hinky"—I have no idea where that name came from; it just is
33. "Charts and Darts" is a reference to a chart that is a large piece of graph paper, and the darts are multicolored pins used to represent locations of the firing unit, the target, and the observer

My new battery commander was really an unknown factor in this whole situation. I didn't know whether he would back me up or rip my head off. He had grown up in a cannon unit as a young LT and had spent some time as a fire support officer in an attack aviation unit (also known as "Apaches" or "AH-64s"). I really didn't know how much he knew about the MLRS system or how much of a kiss-ass he was going to be. When I called him, I gave him a shortened version of the story. He told me he had just gotten off the phone with the XO, and the XO had chewed his ass. He told me to come to his office and lay out the whole scenario. I told the other LTs and the NCOIC they were on their own, as I had to go and deal with this XO business. As I walked out of the FDC, the NCO followed me and asked if I needed any backup. I said, "Thanks" but told him he needed to finish training, and if I needed him, I'd let him know later. Trying to think positive thoughts, I drove to the commander's office.

When I arrived at the battery commander's office, I sat down, and he asked me to explain the whole story. I laid it out as best I could. He asked me if I thought the others involved would back up my story. I told him what the NCO had said as I'd walked away. About that time the phone rang, and the battalion commander asked for our side of the story. The battery commander told the battalion commander he'd be right there, hung up the phone, and told me to stand fast, as he'd be right back.

About an hour later, the battery commander returned and told me everything had been put back right. I asked him what had happened. Here's what he told me.

As he walked into the battalion headquarters building, he heard the XO still hollering about the disrespectful way he'd been treated, saying, "There isn't any way an LT would throw me out of training." He was slamming things down on his desk and generally making an ass of himself. The battery commander walked into the battalion commander's office and sat down, and the battalion commander asked what had happened. The battery commander laid it all out on the table and emphasized the fact that the XO had thrown the manual at the LT first. The battalion commander called the XO into the office and told him to sit down. He looked him straight in the eye and told him he wasn't to attend any more training events without the battery commander at his side.

The XO asked what was to be done about that disrespectful LT who had thrown him out of training, "How dare he say I'm not in his food chain!" he barked. The battalion commander replied coolly, "You're not.

Now go cool off. If I hear anything else about this, you'll be looking for a new job."

After hearing this I breathed a sigh of relief. I'd thought I was a goner for sure. I headed back to the training site to assist with putting everything away for the night and to ensure my platoon had completed the safety computation for the live fire. When I returned, everything was just about put away, and they had figured out their glitch. Safety really isn't that hard once the system is working properly—and when XOs stay out of our business.

UNDERCOVER

NOW I KNOW THIS STORY ISN'T REALLY A SOLDIER STORY, HOWEVER, IT happened to me while I was a soldier so I added it for its entertainment value alone.

Several years ago, my brother-in-law and I were hanging out in Austin together. He was a Texas State Trooper working undercover narcotics at the time. We had hit a few bars earlier and we were feeling a bit buzzed so we decided to pop into a Taco Bell for a snack and give us a little time to sober up before we headed home.

As we finished our snack and started sipping come coffee, a couple of kids (three to be exact) walked through the doors, talking rather loudly. It was rather obvious that all three kids had gone to high school together. One was obviously going to college in Austin and the other two were visiting. They ordered their meals, headed over to a table near us, and continued talking rather loudly about their exploits.

The kid who was attending college in Austin was bragging about all the parties he had gone to so my brother-in-law walked over, sat down next to them, and started chatting with him. My brother-in-law began to pump this kid for information, everything from places he had been, people he had met, phone numbers, addresses, everything, and anything to do with drugs, underage drinking, etc. My brother-in-law was as charming as he could be.

After a few minutes, the kid got up and headed over to the restrooms. As soon as he was out of sight, my brother-in-law reached into his back pocket, pulled out his badge, and set it on the table. The smile was gone from his face and he stared at the other two kids without a shred of emotion in his eyes. The silence in the room was deafening. I could see the fear in their eyes and could almost hear their hearts racing as time seemed to stand still.

About five minutes later, the braggart returned from the restroom. My brother-in-law picked up his badge and returned it to his back pocket as he stood up. The charm had returned to his face and he shook the kid's hand saying we had to get going. "Maybe I'll see you at one of these parties," my brother-in-law said.

"We're headed to one now," the kid replied, "Maybe you and your friend can join us."

"No, we really have to get going." With that, he walked back over to our table and we headed out the door. I think I bit a hole in my lip trying not to laugh my ass off…

COL RED BULL

THIS STORY IS ABOUT A MAN I MET WHEN I WAS A SECOND LIEUTENANT while at Fort Sill, Oklahoma, in the late 1990's. Our battalion commander wanted to reconnect with some of the former leaders of our battalion, had tracked some down, and had coordinated a series of Officer Professional Developments (OPDs) so we might learn from some of their experiences. One of them called himself COL Red Bull. This was in no way plagiarism of the famous energy drink as the OPD happened about the time that the energy drink was first introduced to this country. Truthfully, I had never heard of the drink until years after I met this retired colonel.

The reason he called himself COL Red Bull, had everything to do with the fact his last name was Bull and he, at least at one point, had flaming red hair. By the time I met him he was in his late fifties or early sixties so a lot of his hair had already turned white, but you could see traces of red hiding in there somewhere. He wasn't all that tall or foreboding. He was from a small town in Oklahoma I had never heard of before and talked much like a country bumpkin. Although he wasn't exactly fat, he had a small pot belly as being retired for a couple of years he had long giving up on his physical training. One could tell he had a rare intelligence about him and even though he had retired as a colonel, he didn't seem like one of those over-educated pecker heads one runs into these days. He looked like he would be more at home driving a tractor while plowing a field as he would be sitting behind a desk or leading soldiers across a battlefield.

What struck me as interesting about COL Bull was the story he told about his tour in Vietnam. Apparently, sometime in the mid-sixties, he had just received his commission as an artillerist on active duty and was sent to Vietnam as a platoon leader leading a platoon of 105mm howitzers. The Army had just developed a new "beehive" round in an effort to stop firebases from being overrun by the enemy. A "beehive" round is kinda like a shotgun shell for an artillery piece. The round is designed to explode almost immediately upon exiting the tube (or barrel) of the gun and spread out in a wall of flechettes. Flechettes are little steel projectiles flying at a high rate of speed, intended to shred whatever comes in contact with them. Like I said, it's more or less like a shotgun round, except a lot bigger and a lot more deadly.

There were only four of these rounds in the East Asian theater and all four were issued to young 2LT Bull. He was told in no uncertain terms he was not to fire these rounds because they were part of an experiment. He was to wait until the research team was present so they could witness the rounds being fired for posterity. 2LT Bull put the rounds at the back of his cache and vowed not to fire them until told to.

A couple of weeks ran by and, truthfully, he had forgotten about these special rounds in the back of his cache until one day when all hell broke loose. I think he told us it was right around the time of the Tet Offensive and his fire base was under extreme duress. His gunners had fired every round out of his cache and he was going black[34] on ammo. As they fired the last of his rounds the enemy continued to press their attack. He looked in the back of his cache site and saw those four rounds sitting there on the floor. He made a quick decision that would ultimately change his career forever. He ordered his gunners to fire the beehive rounds. The resulting mayhem stopped the onslaught and ultimately saved the firebase. But, 2LT Bull just knew his career was over. He had fired the rounds.

Instead of being a goat he was a hero. He had used the rounds at the last possible moment and turned the tide of the attack. He thought he would be relieved and sent to some horrible assignment and instead, everyone with half a name wanted to shake his hand. I think he received the Silver Star for his actions. I remember as he was telling this story he paused for a second, shrugged his shoulders and said, "Who knew I would be a hero for disobeying orders."

This isn't the end of the story of COL Bull. He continued by telling us that the rest of his career was more or less plain-Jane with nothing out of the ordinary. He expected to be asked to resign on several occasions mostly due to what he thought was incompetence. He knew that he wasn't always the best guy for the job but for some reason he kept on being offered jobs of importance and prestige. The only thing he could

---

34. Being "black" is army speak for being out of or almost out of anything crucial. Be it ammo, fuel, food, etc.

attribute for receiving such recognition was those beehive rounds he fired in Vietnam.

Eventually, he was offered the opportunity to command a battalion. He knew that everyone on the battalion staff was smarter, or at least more educated, than he was and he didn't want to appear to be dumb. So, he just kept his mouth shut and when someone asked him a question, he would just grumble, shake his head, and walk away. He said he was able to dodge everything important by acting like he was too busy to deal with their trivial issues.

After he had been in command for about eight weeks he remembered sitting down at a staff meeting. He and his staff had been going at it for about an hour or so and he had grumbled several times. He admitted to being more than a little bored (claiming he had nodded off a time or two) when he noticed the room had more or less gone silent. He slowly looked around the room, eyeballing every officer in the room, and not knowing exactly why everyone was staring at him. They all sat there in silence for a few moments when his executive officer leaned over to him and said, "Sir, their waiting on your guidance."

Guidance, damn, he would have to talk now. COL Bull was afraid that everyone would see through his façade and that they would see him as a fraud. He really didn't know what to say or what to do. Without trying to appear too incompetent, he again looked at everyone and said, "Meet me in my office at 0600 tomorrow morning and I'll have your guidance." With that, he stood up and exited the room as fast as he could. He went straight to his office and sat down behind his desk.

"'Guidance," he thought. "What guidance can I give that room full of intelligent officers that they don't already know?"

He pondered this question all night while sitting at his desk.

0600 rolled around faster than he would have liked. As the young officers under his command gathered in his office he still didn't know exactly what he would tell them. Eventually the executive officer reported all officers were accounted for and were standing by for his guidance.

Once again he sat there and eyeballed everyone. Suddenly, he stood up and walked over to a chalk board he had in his office. He picked up a piece of chalk and drew a large circle. Inside that circle he drew a smaller one. Inside that circle he drew yet another one. Finally, in the center of the concentric circles he drew a bull's eye. He then turned around and pointing to the bull's eye in his best command voice he said,

"Maintenance, training, and personnel. That's your bull's eye. Everything else is bullshit."

He placed the chalk back down, walked back over to his desk, and sat down. Everyone just sat there and looked at him.

"Dismissed." He growled.

With that everyone piled out of his office. He was quite certain that wasn't the guidance they were looking for but that was all he would give them. He must have had a successful command because he eventually was promoted. He ultimately served his country for 28 years before he decided to retire. I hope he is still alive, living there in that small Oklahoma town. The world needs men of his brilliance.

THE BATTALION COMMANDER

I WANTED TO PREFACE THIS NEXT STORY WITH A DISCLAIMER. THIS IS JUST a story about a commander I knew who had an extreme sense of humor. I personally don't care about another person's sexual orientation. Homosexuality is not for me. Because of where I was raised, and the way I was raised, if I were to see two of my male lieutenants dancing at a ball, I would probably freak out. It's just who I am. So, if you are offended easily because of a person's different views towards sexual orientation, then I suggest you skip this story.

One of the battalion commanders within the brigade was a real character. He seemed to have a good sense of humor and wasn't one of those who only wanted the jokes to go one way. I have met plenty of the other types, you know, they play a joke on you then get mad when you reciprocate…assholes. Anyway, this battalion commander, like most, would hold staff meetings according to a regular schedule. Normally there are three types of regular meetings for a battalion; there are training meetings, staff call, and command and staff.

Battalion commanders rarely attend training meetings. Training meetings are really training and resourcing meetings. The battalion commander generally leaves the conduct of this type of meeting with his training officer, or S3 (Operations). The S3 is normally a major and he has a staff of captains, lieutenants, and staff NCOs who coordinate and resource the battalion's missions, training, etc. The purpose of the meeting is to coordinate with the battalion's subordinate units and ensure their needs are met.

Staff Call is when the battalion commander's staff briefs him on staff actions ongoing, issues they are having, and staff actions requiring the commanders' attention—meaning they have taken the issue as far as they can and the commander needs to get involved or the matter (whatever it is) is a dead issue[35]. The staff sections are labeled S1 through S9[36]. Each section has a function within the unit. The more common sections are:

S1 Personnel Management or PAC (Personnel Actions Center). They handle all paperwork from individual evaluations[37], awards, to an individual's pay.

S2 Intelligence. They handle security clearances, maps, and analyze the enemy's potential actions.

S3 Training, as previously stated, handles the planning and coordination of the different training events.

S4 Logistics who handles the logistics and the property for the unit.

S6 Communications who handles the communications and computers for the unit.

There are other sections, the S5 Planning, S7 Pysops, S8 Finance, and S9 Civil Affairs . At the battalion and brigade level, these sections aren't generally staffed until the unit deploys to a war zone[38].

Command and Staff is when the subordinate units report their status to the commander. Generally the subordinate commanders, their senior NCO, and the battalion commander's staff attends these meetings so they can explain or react to something briefed or, in some cases, not briefed.

I explained all that so I could get to the root of this story. This battalion commander would bring a water pistol into these meetings, and if the battalion commander had an issue with something a staff member

---

35. A good example of this is, let's say for example the unit wants to train in a particular training area and the training area is currently in use by another unit. Let's assume the two training officers can't come to an agreement on the terms of the co-use. The training officer then brings this issue to the attention of the commander who then decides to engage the commander of the other unit or he gives guidance to use a different training area.

36. At Battalion or Brigade level the different sections are designated with an "S." I have no idea what the "S" stands for but I think it stands for "Staff." At Division and Corps levels the sections are designated with a "G", and I'm guess that stands for "General Staff." At levels above Corps, the sections are labeled with a "J", and, again guessing, that stands for "Joint." To be "Joint" means there are folks from the different branches of the military, Army, Air Force, or Navy working in or around the section.

37. Officer Evaluations Reports (OERs) or Non-Commissioned Officer Evaluation Reports (NCOERs)

38. At the time of the writing of this book there has been a recent push to staff these sections prior to deploying. My gut feeling is that as soon as the army starts feeling the squeeze on its budget, these sections will once again go unmanned until absolutely needed.

briefed, the commander would pull out the water pistol and commence to spraying the briefer. When he first did this, everyone was in a state of shock. After six months, it was considered a badge of honor to walk out of the meeting drenched. The XO, one day, decided to get even with the battalion commander so he coordinated to have super soakers stashed underneath everybody's chair. On cue, everyone was to pull out his or her super soaker and drench the commander.

The commander walked into the meeting, and as customary, the meeting began. About five minutes into the meeting as the commander began to spray a briefer, the XO gave the signal and everybody pulled out their soakers and drenched the battalion commander. After that, the meeting descended into a free-for-all. The meeting wasn't very productive but it was one of the best meetings I've ever heard of.

I'll bet the reader is wondering, what does this have to do with two boys having sex? I wanted to establish the command environment before I got to the meat and potatoes of this story. So, without further ado…

The commander's favorite saying was, "That's as wrong as two boys fuckin.'" He used it almost too often and often he would use it in inappropriate situations. It seemed as if he really didn't care who was around him—a chaplain, a female officer—it didn't seem to matter. Sometimes it was almost embarrassing, but somehow, with his personality, he was able to pull it off without getting in trouble.

After he had been in command for about a year or so, his S1, decided to play a prank on him. After hours, the S1 snuck into the commander's office and replaced one of the pictures hanging on the wall behind the desk with a picture of two men having sex. The commander never noticed it. After several weeks, the S1 forgot about the picture and everything more or less chugged along without incident.

One day, the commander had a meeting in order to interview a new chaplain for the battalion. So, the chaplain arrived at the commander's office and reported as protocol[39] required. The commander returned the chaplain's salute. The picture on the wall behind the commander's desk was almost the first thing the chaplain noticed.

The chaplain, being rather embarrassed, really didn't know what to do so he decided to play it coy and avoid staring at the picture. The commander noticed the chaplain's discomfort and after five or ten

---

39. The protocol for a reporting officer is to stand in front of the commander's desk and salute and saying, "Sir, So and so reporting as ordered."

minutes of the chaplain avoiding the commander's gaze the commander said, "What the hell is wrong!?"

"Uh, Sir, the picture behind your desk, it's, uh, rather inappropriate," the chaplain stammered.

"What picture!?!" The commander snapped as he turned around.

"What the Hell!!! S1, get your ass in here!!!"

Afterwards, everyone had a pretty good laugh.

THE FUNERAL DETAIL

ONE OF GREATEST HONORS GIVEN TO AN OFFICER IS TO BE CALLED UPON to act as the army's representative at a fallen soldier's funeral—to offer a final farewell and a salute to the surviving family members. I was given this honor on several occasions. I must say my most difficult funeral was the first, but it wasn't the most memorable one.

In order to set up this story I must explain a few things. As far as I know, there are two types of army funerals. There is full honors and a funeral rep (short for "represent"). A full honors funeral is the one most folks associate with military funerals. A full honors funeral often as few as eight soldiers; six pallbearers who also act as guards of honor featuring five rifleman and one NCO directing them, the officer and the NCOIC of the team. What happens is a full team shows up, acts as pallbearers, folds the draped flag off the coffin, and fires a three-round salute to the fallen. Incidentally, this is mistakenly known as a 21 gun salute. The salute is three rounds as in saying good-bye three times; the number of weapons used is really immaterial. After the three round salute, the senior NCO and the officer gracefully fold the flag and the officer then places three rounds (generally empty brass casings) into the flag and offers it to the next of kin offering a six second salute.

In contrast, a funeral rep is only two soldiers—an NCO, and an officer. They fold the draped flag, and the officer offers it to the next of kin. If a soldier were to die while on active duty or retired from active duty, the family may request a full honors funeral; if a soldier serves a length of service but does not retire, then the family may request a funeral rep. Truth is, my personal belief is every soldier desires a full honors funeral, however, due to a lack of resources, what we have is what we have. I digress…

I was sent to Fort Smith, Arkansas in order to perform a funeral rep. As I would normally do, in order to be prepared, I would arrive at the funeral location a day prior and do a recon of the area, meet with the funeral director, and find a hotel as close as possible to the funeral home.

This time things went about as normal as ever. My NCO and I then performed our drill by the numbers and without a hitch. By the time the NCO and I finished the funeral it was too late to head back to Fort Sill, so we decided to stay the night. That evening, I received a call from headquarters and was given another funeral rep for the next day. As we were already in Arkansas, it was more economical to leave us at Fort Smith instead of sending a new team. The funeral was in Booneville, Arkansas. Booneville was near Fort Smith and being that it was already pretty late, the NCO and I decided to forego the normal recon and link up with the funeral director in the morning.

We woke up earlier than normal and headed out to Booneville. Once we arrived, we started looking for the funeral home. None of the directions seemed to make sense. None of the street names matched. About 0800 (8 AM for the civilians) I frantically called the funeral home to ask for better directions. As hard as the funeral director and I tried to make sense of the directions we were unsuccessful.

Finally, he said, "From the sounds of it you're down near Fort Smith."

"Yes, we are about an hour outside of Fort Smith in the town of Booneville," I said.

"Oh, that's the problem. The funeral is not in Booneville, it's in Boone County."

Holy Shit! Boone County was about 3 hours up the road. It was currently 0800 and the funeral was at 1000. There was no way in hell we could make the funeral in time. By the way, if a funeral team messes up a funeral, the word will get back to the chain of command. When this occurs, it isn't a fun day.

I had never screwed up a funeral, much less been late or missed one to which I was assigned. I told the director we would make it. I looked at my NCO and gave one simple command, "Drive." We had the van we were driving pegged out as we hit the highway. Our speeds well exceeded 120mph. I knew that if we missed the funeral we were screwed, if we were pulled over and given a ticket, we were screwed, and, if we were arrested for unsafe driving, we were screwed. The only way this could turn out good was with a little bit of luck. About an hour or so later my NCO saw flashing whoopee lights in his rear view mirror.

"Uh, Sir, what should I do?" he asked (remember the definition of a good driver? I always had the best).

"Slow down," I replied, "maybe he will see our government plates and give us the benefit of the doubt."

So, my NCO slowed down and a highway patrolman pulled up beside us and motioned to roll down the window.

"Ya'll the ones headed to the Boone County Funeral home?" He hollered.

"Y-y-yes," my NCO responded.

"Follow me!"

Again, Holy Shit! What luck! A police escort. We fell in behind the highway patrolman and sped up the road. I climbed in the back of the vehicle and began to change into my dress uniform. Once I was dressed, I traded seats with my NCO as he changed; all this while speeding down the road at speeds up to 120 mph—safe? Hell no, but we both figured it was better to explain an accident than a failed funeral.

We pulled into the cemetery, found an out of the way parking spot, and climbed out of the van minutes before the funeral procession arrived. As far as any of the family members knew, we were waiting there for them. We performed the ceremony to perfection. Afterwards, I linked up with the highway patrolman and was given the rest of the story. He was the brother-in-law to the funeral director. The funeral director had called him and sent him out to find us and bring us in.

THE METH HEAD

SEVERAL MONTHS HAD PASSED AND THINGS PRETTY MUCH CHUGGED along without much incident. The Army, in all it benevolence, generally plans a long weekend (most times a four day) once a month. Sometimes, we got a couple of long weekends. As a matter of fact, from the beginning of November until the end of February, if one were to count the actual duty days and compare them to DONSA's[40] one would discover more time off duty than on.

Some commanders, rightfully so, have adopted the practice of conducting a urinalysis after a long weekend in order to deter the use of illicit drugs. The army urinalysis program is just that, a deterrence program designed with the intent to scare folks off of using drugs and from time to time catching a user. The way I see it is, there should be no reason for anyone using drugs. The only purpose for drug use is as a form of escapism. If, for some reason, you don't like your life then in my opinion do something to change your life so you don't have to escape from it. Well, enough parenting I suppose…back to the story.

After a long weekend, the commander conducted a urinalysis and I was surprised when my FDNCOs got a hit with meth use. The alleged offender had been a very good performer and the thought of him using meth was unbelievable. He was called in and asked how this could be possible[41].

The FDNCO claimed his wife was a known user of meth and she liked to dissolve the meth in a glass of water and he thought it was possible he consumed some of this water unknowingly. Given his past work

---

40. DONSA—Day Of No Scheduled Activity. Basically, a day off.

41. You see, in order to be prosecuted for drug use a Soldier needs to knowingly take the drug. What this means is, if a Soldier is at a party and someone decides to slip a little something into his drink and the Soldier drinks it, then he can't be held liable. This is almost never the case. In fact I would estimate 99 times out of a 100 this is not the case, however in the case of my FDNCO this seemed plausible.

performance, we (the chain of command) thought this was plausible. So, we approached the battalion commander with his explanation. Normally, the battalion commander reserves the right to handle the UCMJ in most drug related incidents. With this explanation and the FDNCO's prior performance, the battalion commander agreed the story was believable. So, the battalion commander decided to put the NCO on probation for six months meaning, as long as the NCO kept his act clean, nothing would happen.

It had taken about a month or so to set up the meeting with the battalion commander. That morning of the meeting the battery commander had planned another urinalysis. It takes anywhere from about four days to a week to get the results of a urinalysis. Lo and behold, the same FDNCO scored another hit for meth use. What the hell?

Although I don't remember the exact amount, I remember being told that the amount of drugs in his urine would indicate the FDNCO was probably out in the parking lot snorting (or smoking) meth minutes before the drug test. So, once again he was brought in and we put the screws to him (figuratively). At this point he decided to plead the 5th amendment (yes, even soldiers have rights) so we got him hooked up with a lawyer to defend his current alleged drug use. The original charge (the one he was placed on probation with) we used to demote him.

This character went from saint to shit bag in a matter of minutes. Once a soldier is a suspected drug user, the chain of command turns a keen eye towards his or her activities. In other words, the suspected drug user is almost always selected for drug screening. All told, this FDNCO was tested six times for drug use over six months and tested positive for meth use six times. In other words, he was probably using it just about every day.

Apparently, he came clean to one of his buddies about his story. It was true his wife was a known meth user. The FDNCO claimed he confronted his wife about her use and insisted she stop—cold turkey. She responded that it wasn't that easy to quit and she wanted help. He was embarrassed about her use and didn't want it publicly known so he told her she had to stop cold. He wanted to prove to her that it was easy to stop, so one night he took a hit off her pipe, then another, and so on. Next thing you know he was addicted.

He ended up with six months in a federal jail for his blatant disregard for the army's anti-drug policy.

THE PLATOON SERGEANT

DRUGS HAVE BEEN A PROBLEM IN THE ARMY FOR AS LONG AS I CAN REMEMBER. Why folks think they can get away with using drugs while on active duty I'll never understand. The urinalysis may not catch a user the first, second, or even the third time; but the odds are against the user and eventually the user will be caught. It's just not worth it.

In another battery within my battalion, the battery commander was a good friend of mine. He told me this story about a platoon sergeant who, the morning of a urinalysis, approached the 1SG and informed him of his prior drug use. Apparently, the night before the platoon sergeant had partied it up and consumed a large quantity of meth. The platoon sergeant had the understanding that if he admitted to using drugs before a urinalysis he was untouchable.

Truth is, that is kinda true. What I mean is, if a soldier admits to having a substance abuse problem this is called a "self-referral." However, the morning of a urinalysis, after being informed about the urinalysis, trying self-referral is too late. You're caught! Incidentally, I do remember a different soldier who did a self-referral for ecstasy use. We were able to get him help and as far as I know he made a successful recovery. I digress.

So, this platoon sergeant unsuccessfully tried a self-referral and the battery chain of command began the process of UCMJ, so, nothing new there…unless you count a visit by CID (Criminal Investigation Division) later in the week, as normal. CID is a unit within the army who is kinda like IA (Internal Affairs) for the police. CID agents are like military police on steroids. They work for a General in Washington so they are outside the local chain of command. Most of them are plain clothed and you don't see them coming until it's too late.

Anyway, my friend, the battery commander, received a visit from CID and they had an interesting story. Apparently, this platoon sergeant was more than just a user; he was the mastermind behind a drug ring of pushers and dealers on the post. He was using his influence as a platoon sergeant to recruit young and impressionable NCOs into his ring. He started within his platoon and branched out from there. The platoon sergeant's drug ring had been under investigation for weeks. The CID investigation was still ongoing and the agent asked the battery commander to hold off on the UCMJ until they had completed it. CID wanted to get the whole ring and if the platoon sergeant got wind of their investigation, it might scare off the proverbial bigger fish. So, the battery commander agreed to stall for the foreseeable future.

Several weeks went by and nothing happened. There is such a thing as due process in the army, just like in the civilian world, and the battery commander was pushing the threshold with this drug charge. CID wanted to postpone longer in order to bring down the whole ring. By now, everybody in the battery knew of the drug-using platoon sergeant. The commander was concerned if he didn't act fast there would be dire consequences to the good order and discipline within his battery.

I think now is a good time to explain the differences between how criminal charges work in the army as opposed to the civilian world. In the civilian world, anyone can press charges against anyone for just about anything. I am talking about a civil lawsuit as well as criminal as there is such a thing as a "citizen's arrest." In the army there is nothing like a civil law suit nor a citizen's arrest. As far as criminal charges go, the state, as well as the common citizen, can press charges against anyone who has violated the law. In the army, the only one who can press charges against a soldier is a commander within in the soldier's chain of command. If you haven't gathered it by now, there are several levels within the chain of command. Remember, CID is not within the chain of command…they are outside. So, they can only investigate, not press charges.

Some civilians are thinking how does this all work? Well, truth is, I am not a military lawyer so I don't know the ins and outs of the whole system. Trust me, it works. CID does the investigation and the commander charges the accused. By the way, soldiers are still accountable to civilian law as well as military law, and, if the civilian law charges a soldier, he can't be charged for the same crime in the military. However, there is always article 134, the last article of the punitive codes in the UCMJ. We call this one the catchall. Without going into too much detail, just about anything a soldier does that the commander doesn't like is punishable under this code. Lawyers probably want to argue this point. If you do, swing by and we'll talk about it over a beer.

Anyway, the battery commander won out against CID and the decision to act against known members of the drug ring was made. So, now the problem was how to get all the members of the ring together in the same location and bring them down in one fell swoop? The army's answer? Since most of the drug ring came from the same battery, hold a formation.

1SG put out a list of names of soldiers who were going to receive awards. The list happened to coincide with the ones who were members of the drug ring. The day of the awards ceremony arrived. The awardees were called out in front of the battery. The signal was given. CID agents and MPs came rushing out of their hiding positions…and the rest is history.

APOCALYPTIC POOP

THE NEXT BIG FIELD EXERCISE I WAS A PART OF AS A PLATOON LEADER WAS when we deployed to Twentynine Palms, California. Some folks will ask, what the heck is an army artillery unit doing on a Marine post? We were an MLRS battalion (Multiple Launch Rocket System—and we shoot really far!). We needed space to shoot our systems and Twentynine Palms was just about perfect because the entire post is an impact zone. We loved it. Anyway, we had been there for about a week or so and I had my platoon set up in a platoon operating area. I was driving around early one morning looking over some things when an urge in my bowels hit me.

I told my driver to stop the vehicle and I climbed out, grabbed the shovel, the toilet seat, and walked around to the front of the vehicle. I then dropped the grill on the hummer, clamped the toilet seat to the grill, and dug a hole directly under the seat. I climbed on the seat and began to read. My driver, having a bit more couth, walked around to the rear of the hummer to smoke a cigarette.

Unbeknownst to me, my platoon sergeant saw my humvee from a distance. Not knowing what I was up to, he decided the area I had picked to do my duty was a good place to feed chow. He approached my vehicle from the backside and was oblivious to my disposition.

Our normal procedure for feeding chow was for the platoon sergeant to call the launcher chiefs and have them meet us at a centralized location, back the two humvees together, drop the tailgates so he would have two flat surfaces to serve chow from.

Imagine my surprise when I heard the tell-tale sounds of approaching tracked vehicles and right in front of me there was one screaming towards my position. As the launcher approached I saw the launcher chief pointing and laughing his butt off. I looked to my left and saw another launcher approaching, this chief had his camera out and was snapping photos for posterity. This is a situation they really don't train you on at

OBC (Officer Basic Course). I did what every good leader would do in this situation…I reached for the toilet paper.

I had to live through a myriad of jokes thrown at me about this incident. One of my favorites was, "Hey, I knew army chow tasted like shit, but I didn't know where it really came from." To say the least, I was the "butt" of everybody's joke for the next couple of weeks. One of those pictures ended up in the After Action Report. Was I embarrassed? Hell, no! It's just that I thought my ass was a little hairier.

WIFE TO THE RESCUE... AGAIN

SOON AFTER THE DRUG USER INCIDENT, I RECEIVED A NEW FDNCO. THIS new fella was another real piece of work. He looked like a quintessential North Carolina hillbilly National Guardsman, like he'd crawled out of the Blue Ridge Mountains right into the army. He was missing all his front teeth, and the ones he had left looked like they were about rotten. Let me tell you, he showed up as a real braggart, claiming he had singlehandedly defeated Saddam Hussein's army in Desert Shield/Desert Storm (the First Gulf War). I doubt he was even in the army at that time. Nonetheless he was trouble from the word go. His typical excuse for not being able to complete an assigned task had something to do with an aliment or two he had picked up while in Desert Shield/Desert Storm.

We were still doing the field-training exercise (FTX) in Twentynine Palms, California. Prior to the deployment while we were doing the train up for this FTX, this new FDC chief was trying everything he could think of to get out of the FTX. His most successful ailment was carpal tunnel syndrome. The neurologist had this guy on a "dead man's profile," meaning he couldn't do much more activity than a dead man. My new PSG and I decided we wanted to make an example of this guy. We both thought he was malingering, so I talked to the battalion physician's assistant (PA)[42], regarding our options. She (there weren't many women in a field-artillery battalion during this time; she was one of a kind) called the neurologist and explained that this character was a "must have" for the field. What could she do to help him not injure himself further so we could get him to the field? The neurologist gave her some advice, and she went to work.

---

42. Most anyone associated with the medical profession is referred to as "Doc" from the combat medic to an actual Medical Doctor.

When she was done with this guy, both his arms were bandaged up like a tampon. All that was missing was the string. His arms shot out in front of him, and he was required to wear this apparatus at all times, except while showering. Since we didn't have many showers in the field, it wouldn't pose much of a problem. He wore that thing for about two days. After that he decided his ailment wasn't that bad.

About two weeks into the field exercise, I received an urgent message to call my wife. As we weren't supposed to have cell phones while in the field I didn't have a phone on me at the time. I received the message through the Family Readiness Group (or FRG—a group normally made up of spouses and generally led by one of the more senior spouses). The group supports each other while the soldiers are off playing army. The battalion's FRG was led by the battalion commander's wife. The message I received was on a little piece of paper. It didn't have a whole lot of information as all it said was, "Call me."

My battery commander had a government cell phone, and as this was an urgent request, he let me use his phone. I called my wife, and she told me one sorry story. This knucklehead (the malingering FDC chief) had left his wife and three kids at home with $100 and no car and had taken her ID with him. He also had told his wife not to call anyone unless it was an emergency. He didn't tell her how long we'd be gone for the field exercise (about thirty-five days) or who to contact to find out this information.

Since we had been at Twenty-nine Palms for a couple of weeks and she only had $100 his wife had run out of food, and the water had been shut off, she figured her current situation constituted an emergency. So she found my wife's phone number in a pile of paperwork and called her. My wife immediately organized the spouses and headed over to her house. They brought her enough food for the duration of the field exercise and arranged for the water to be turned back on. My wife said she'd never seen such a sorry sight in her life—those poor kids and that spouse having to put up with that situation.

My new PSG went to work on this FDC chief. Although the guy deserved it, he didn't get his ass beaten (several folks volunteered), but my PSG did ride his ass hard and went out to check on the family every week from the time we went home to the time that ass PCS'ed from the battery. The PSG went so far as to buy the wife a cell phone and told her to hide it and to call him or his wife if the knucklehead tried anything. Some folks don't deserve the blessings bestowed upon them.

FREAKED OUT!

ANOTHER BIZARRE CHARACTER I RAN INTO WAS THE NBC[43] NCO OF OUR battery. When I first met him I knew something was off about this guy but I couldn't quite place it. I mean, he had a wife, a couple of kids, and seemed to have his stuff together, but something just seemed a bit off. After knowing him for several months, I did notice that he had false teeth. All of them. I had known folks in the past to have all their teeth pulled for one reason or another, but, those folks were generally older and as this guy was in his mid-twenties, I thought that was rather strange. I never really got the chance to ask him about his teeth and why they had been removed…but I found out another way that made shivers run up and down my spine.

Sometime in the mid-nineties, President Clinton had spearheaded the "Don't Ask, Don't Tell" policy. My father's generation is generally freaked out by homosexuals. My generation, well, we mostly don't care one way or another but, I would still be freaked out if I saw two of my male lieutenants dancing together in a loving manner at a battalion ball. Of course, the current policy (as of the writing of this book) is, it doesn't matter whether or not a guy or gal is gay. The army accepts all. Now, my son's generation is more accepting of homosexuals. They really don't care one way or another. He and I haven't really talked about how he would feel in a group shower situation with folks of different sexual orientation, just to be clear—you find yourself in these situations in the army from time to time.

This NCO? Well, he kept his little secret pretty well to himself for the most part. What do I mean for the most part? One Saturday afternoon his wife had invited all the spouses to her house as a "family team building" exercise. Army Family Team building was started a long time ago and

---

43. NBC stands for Nuclear, Biological, and Chemical—The NBC NCO at the battery level is the expert on how to deal with these unfortunate situations…scary

only recently (the past four to five years as of the writing of this book) has it become a professional course for some folks, but back in the late nineties it was on an all-volunteer basis. My battery commander had made it a point to make the Family Readiness Group (FRG) a priority and the spouses had agreed to shift the burden of hosting the monthly meetings among themselves. I guess the NBC NCO's wife either forgot to tell her husband, he really didn't care, or he had forgotten about the meeting all together. But the day of the meeting the spouses were in for the shock of their lives.

As the group of spouses knocked on the door, the ugliest woman they had ever seen answered. She had an unshaven shadow and was wearing an ill-fitting dress. She played at hostess all afternoon which leads one to think it was a planned occurrence all along. A couple of the NCOs had attended with their spouses and they kept thinking the unknown woman looked a lot like the NBC NCO. Maybe it was a twin sister with a hormone problem. It wasn't until one of the spouses accidently walked in on the unknown woman in the bathroom and saw her standing and peeing that all hell broke loose. Yes, if you haven't figured it out yet, it was the NBC NCO dressed in drag. The unsuspecting spouse freaked out, screamed, and ran into the living room where everyone else was more or less concerned.

The NBC NCO walked into the living room, removed his wig, and just stood there. I don't think anyone really knew how to react, but I know everyone pretty much high-tailed it out of there lickety-split. Now, I don't know for sure if he was actually a homosexual. He may have been bisexual or just liked to dress in drag. I guess it really doesn't matter ultimately; it was just a weird way to come out of whatever closet he was in. As for having no teeth well, it was rumored that he had them purposely removed as an aid to oral sex. Eeewww…

MAKE IT SO!

EVENTUALLY I BECAME THE SENIOR LIEUTENANT IN THE BATTERY. I GUESS I should explain that statement. In those days, a normal MLRS battery had four lieutenants. Two platoon leaders, one support platoon leader, and one operations officer. Generally speaking, the newer lieutenants are given platoons so the platoon sergeants can begin to train them on the ins and outs of being an officer in the army. The next senior lieutenant is given the support platoon. This slot is give or take. Normally, the support platoon is co-located with the battery headquarters element so if the battery is short lieutenants; the support position is left empty. The most senior lieutenant is the battery operations officer and is, as far as I know, the only staff officer in a battery sized element.

Now is probably a good time to explain more or less each officer's responsibility within a battery while in the field. In a nut shell, the "leaders" recon and the staff officers/platoon sergeants move the battery around the battlefield. So, once a movement order is received from battalion, the battery commander immediately issues a preliminary operations order, then he kicks out for a recon of the new operations area. Each of the platoon leaders upon receiving the preliminary operations order begin movement of their own and they to kick out on recons of their proposed operations area. Somewhere along the way they link up with the battery commander to finalize coordination.

The operations officer and the support platoon leader generally have their hands full. The support platoon leader is leading convoys back and forth between the support "trains" bringing supplies forward and requests for support back to battalion. The operations officer is collapsing the battery operations center and preparing it for movement—all along maintaining the ability to support the maneuver forces with artillery fires. This is generally achieved by echeloning or "leap frogging" the platoons.

At the platoon level, once the platoon leader has completed his recon he links up with his platoon sergeant at a predetermined location.

Behind the platoon sergeant are all the launchers, the FDC, and whatever support vehicles are forward at that point. I always liked to keep the survey plotting team[44] with me when I was a platoon leader for their unique skills at pinpointing my location in order to make my launchers that much more accurate. For some reason, other platoon leaders either because of laziness or apathy just "map spot" locations or used a less accurate plugger (GPS device) for their survey needs. Any old school artillerist will tell you "the more accurate the survey, the more accurate the impact!" Anyway, once the platoon leader and platoon sergeant link up occurs, they switch drivers and the platoon leader leads his launchers to their firing areas as well as emplaces the ammo trucks. The platoon sergeant is taken to the area where the platoon leader has determined the best location for the FDC. The platoon sergeant has the prerogative to move the FDC if the location is indefensible or communications can't be established for one reason or another.

The battery commander does this same procedure but at a higher echelon. In addition to recon and emplacement, the battery commander is constantly on the road back and forth between the battery location, a platoon location, or to battalion in order to receive operational briefs and what not. I'll bet you old NCOs out there are asking, where is the first sergeant in all this? Well, if you run it through MTOE (Modified Table of Organization and Equipment)[45] the first sergeant is located in the back seat with the battery commander as he is not authorized his own vehicle. However, most first sergeants commandeer the NBC NCO's HMMWV and pulls a driver out of the hide from some section of the battery. Most of the time, the first sergeant just uses the NBC NCO for a driver, but not in our case (See the Freaked Out! story). I think our first sergeant was afraid…truly afraid. Anyways, the first sergeant generally has his hands full running chow and dragging the medic all over the area of operations. Additionally, the first sergeant accompanies the battery commander to the battalion operational briefs probably 99% of the time.

In a well-rehearsed and coordinated unit, all this runs seamlessly. I'll bet you civilians out there thought all we did in the field was fish. Not

---

44. The survey plotting team is often referred to as just "survey." They add the much needed element of accuracy to a unit while shooting artillery. There are five requirements of shooting artillery accurately. The first of these is firing unit location. Survey provides this in spades.

45. MTOE is pronounced "M-toe" is the "big army" approved listing of approved equipment and personnel an army unit is authorized to have on hand.

true. Generally speaking, we are on the go probably twenty hours plus out of every day while in the field. Garrison is where we get our rest.

So, now that I was the senior lieutenant in the battery, I sat down with the battery commander and we agreed there was a lot of work needed to get the battery working as a well-oiled machine. One of the areas where we were weakest was when the battery operations center (BOC) was moving. What was supposed to happen is, the operational control of all the launchers was supposed to be transferred over to one of the platoon operations center (POC)–which had the same operational abilities as the BOC. One of the things we agreed to was, we needed to share the wealth when it came to experience. You see, natural progression would ultimately find all the more experienced soldiers in the BOC and leave the POCs high and dry with all the new privates and junior NCOs. No wonder they had trouble assuming control. So, we organized them all into one cohesive unit and gave the sergeant first class in charge of the section the mission of "spread the knowledge." He took the ball and ran with it.

One thing he pointed out was, although the fire direction officer was responsible for things like safety*, there was nothing in the regulation requiring the FDO to do the safety. He just had to approve the safety. So, he made sure all the soldiers in the section were trained and the new TTPs (Tactics, Techniques, and Procedures)[46] he developed was to have the safety data computed by the soldiers under the NCO's supervision.. Then, the NCO would brief the safety data to the officer who would verify the data for accuracy. The officer was still responsible, but he was freed up to "supervise," which is what his job was supposed to be anyway. This also gave the soldiers some "buy in" to the overall operation. It was a win-win situation.

He also pointed out several other things little things we had been overlooking and we developed TTPs around these "little things." With our blessing he trained those fire direction folks to a point where they were as sharp as a tack. When it came to battery certifications, the battalion FDO would test us. Since we were the only ones doing the process our way, the battalion FDO wasn't so sure we would be doing it right. It was only after we beat everybody's time by half and had fewer mistakes that he began to buy in.

During the certification I remember discussing this very subject with

_____

46. TTPs are another way of saying "best practices.'

him. I was being certified as the FDO for the battery and he was telling me that no way in hell should a soldier be responsible to develop safety data. I told him that I was still responsible. The soldiers were just putting the data together. At first, he was telling me that he should fail my section out of principle, when my NCO walked up with the completed safety diagram. The battalion FDO was shocked we had produced it so quickly. But what really won him over was when I pointed out two mistakes on the diagram and the NCO corrected them on the spot. Even with the corrections, we had still beaten the other sections by half the time.

The NCO went back and drilled the soldiers ten more times on safety data after that. Truthfully, the mistakes had been rigged. The reason he rigged it that way was to prove to the battalion guy that even though the soldiers were pulling the numbers together I was still responsible for the data. It worked like a charm. After that, all the other batteries drafted their SOP after ours.

All the training, as it should, paid off in the long run. We were in the field and battalion sent a jump order. I immediately shifted control to one of the platoons and jumped the BOC. Three hours later I reestablished the BOC and the POC jumped in a leap frog maneuver. I remember being so proud once I sent up a closure report[47] and battalion said, "the transition was so smooth we never knew you moved." You see, normally, when a battery jumped there were always issues with the continuation of fires. We had trained past that. That was one highly trained battery.

* Safety with an Artillery battery is paramount. In a nutshell, the safety data is a quick "cheat sheet" giving the launcher chiefs a left and right limit as well as a minimum and maximum quadrant so they are less likely to shoot out or miss the target. The army has reverse engineered this process to a point where all one has to do is add sum, subtract sum, and wham, you have data. The real process is a complicated mess of hyperboles and parabolas with some trigonometry and calculus plugged in for good measure. It took some pretty smart fellas to dumb it down to a point where a monkey leading two lieutenants can figure it out.

---

47. The "closure report" the report saying we were done moving or have finished a particular mission.

MY FIRST BATTALION STAFF JOB

THE BATTALION RETURNED FROM THE FIELD WHERE WE HAD, WELL, JUST kicked ass really. Towards the end of the exercise, both of the other batteries were completely out to lunch for one reason or another. My battery had been the only one operational for the final leg of the exercise. That was one truly well-oiled battery. It was a combination of all of our talents culminating with a good battery commander who knew when to take charge and when to back off and let his subordinates run the show.

Unfortunately, within probably two or three months after we had returned from that deployment the battalion commander had to split the battery up. Not because we had done anything wrong, but the rest of his staff had PCS'd away and he needed replacements. My battery commander became the S3 and I was sent to the S2 (Intelligence) shop.

While in the S2 shop, there were three sergeant first classes and me manning the shop. One was the outgoing NCOIC, one was the incoming NCOIC, and the third was a fella who was retiring in six months or so and they needed to put him somewhere so he was placed in the S2 shop. I don't remember what the required strength of the shop was but I know there wasn't enough work to keep all of us occupied all the time. The NCOs found a way to keep themselves occupied as one thing all three of them had in common was they liked to fish. So with the shop pretty well stocked with personnel, what the three NCOs decided to do was take turns watching the lieutenant. One of them would stay in the shop and the other two would head over to the lake and fish.

This went on for the next couple of months. I knew there wasn't much going on and I never did like to fish much—even being a country boy myself—so I didn't really mind as long as all the work got done. The NCOs never disappointed.

After a couple of months, the battalion commander decided he wanted to test out his new staff so we did what was known as a TWOT[48] (Training With Out Troops). It's pronounced TWOOT for you foul minded folks.... Anyhow, the battalion commander had the S3 dig out an old operations order and we re-engaged it using MDMP (Military Decision Making Process)[49]. This was the first time I had ever done anything like MDMP so this was all new to me. Years later, I can almost do this process in my sleep, but back in those days it seemed overwhelming. Thankfully I had those three NCOs, especially the outgoing one.

You see, the outgoing NCO had been an S2 NCO for many years so he knew the ins and outs of the MDMP process. Additionally, he had known the battalion commander since he had been a young captain so my NCO knew pretty much how the battalion commander would react to a given situation.

During MDMP, at key points, the staff briefs the commander on what they had done with the end state of the brief leading to a decision the commander has to make before the staff can proceed with the next step. I was really nervous for my portion of the brief because I had never done anything like that before, I was not a school trained S2—remember I was an artilleryman, not an intelligence guy—and I really wanted to do a good job. My NCO told me not to worry, he had everything under control.

He put together the brief on Power Point (for some reason the army has fallen in love with this program) and wrote out several note cards. At the brief, I was supposed to read the notecards verbatim and if the commander had any questions, I was to flip the card over where all the answers were. At first I was skeptical, I mean, how the hell did my NCO know what questions the commander would ask. I voiced my concern and the NCO replied, "If you run into any problems just pitch the question back to me. I'll be in the back of the room."

---

48. Training With Out Troops is rather self-explanatory if you ask me, however, for you thick minded folks it's a training exersice where only the staff is engaged. There is never any intent for whatever plan that is developed to actually be executed. Some folks might think this is a waste of time, however, it truly is not. Staff are supposed to analyze and brief the commander. That is our job. The more one practices, as with everything, the better one gets.

49. MDMP is basically a method of looking at a mission and analyzing as many courses of action as possible, in order to give the commander the opportunity to make an informed decision. It is a rather complex process and everybody on the battalion staff has a vital piece.

The day of the brief arrived and I had spent the night memorizing the note cards. When it was my turn to brief I stood up there like a champ and knocked it out of the park. When the commander started to ask questions, I flipped the cards over and lo and behold, my NCO had anticipated every single question. I mean, I had all the answers. I felt like I really knew what I was doing standing up there. After I was finished, the commander gave me a little wink and then he looked over at my NCO and said, "Great brief."

ALL MY SHIT'S BROKE

IN THE SUMMER OF 2002, I RECEIVED PCS ORDERS TO MOVE FROM FORT Sill, Oklahoma, and proceed to Fort Hood, Texas. I was really happy about this because Fort Hood is about two hours from both my wife's and my home town. She and I bought a house and I reported to my new battalion. The battalion XO asked me about my history, and when I mentioned I'd been a mechanic when I was enlisted, he said, "You're my new battalion maintenance officer."

I went to the motor pool and met my team of mechanics and the other staff officers and NCOs. The BMT, who had recently arrived himself, decided we needed to take a look around and assess the situation. He and I walked around the motor pool, went back to our office, and asked our BMS, "Why are all these vehicles in such a shitty state of repair?" The answer was, "They don't care about maintenance."[50] Well, I knew how to make "they" care about maintenance. It was really simple—report the truth. So that's what we did.

With the help of my motor tech, or "Chief"[51], he and I had the mechanics begin a quality assurance/quality control (QA/QC) program and told them to accurately annotate every flaw on a vehicle. After they did this, it was apparent that we'd busted fleet (remember that's when a unit goes below 90 percent on one particular vehicle type), and we'd also busted ALO (the average for all vehicles was below 90 percent). The motor tech warned me not to bust ALO or fleet. I figured the way a wheel gets greased is to squeak. In order to make "they" care about maintenance, I had to paint a bleak picture. So I did. Chief was concerned that the

---

50. In the army, or life for that matter, "they" is often what folks say when they really don't know who to blame. In some cases I do believe there's an international evil organization known as "They."

51. We call techs "Chief," and they're technical experts in whatever their field is; mine one was a maintenance type

squeaky wheel would get replaced. At first he was apprehensive about making the picture too bleak, but he eventually came round to my way of thinking. Besides, if anything really went bad, I was the one to take most of the heat.

Boy, did I get a response. I had folks coming out of the woodwork. There were guys in the motor pool who had never been in the motor pool before. And yes, I did create a lot of work for myself and my staff, but the end result is what I was after—people caring for their vehicles. We had money and parts poured into our motor pool. I had several sets of stars (general officers) visit the motor pool. I think they were more interested in the question of, "Why are you reporting upsetting data?" than how to fix the problem. At any rate, over the course of two or three months, everyone worried about maintenance, and almost everything was fixed.

YOU CAN'T FOOL ME!

I HAD ONE OF THE MOTOR SERGEANTS WALK IN TO MY OFFICE TELLING ME we needed a new transmission for one of the FIST-V's[52]. In my youth, I had been a track vehicle mechanic. I worked on M113's almost exclusively in those days and today, some 20 years later, I can still probably troubleshoot mechanical failures with the best of them on that system. Anyway, when this NCO walked into the office he was adamant about the vehicle needing a transmission.

I asked him a few questions, most notably, "Did you use the manual to troubleshoot the problem?" He got this arrogant look on his face, while saying, "Why do officers always question how we do our job?" Over the next couple of days, my warrant officer and I tracked down a new transmission. We got the transmission in and they set about installing it in the FIST-V.

The next day the same NCO walked into my office and informed me he needed a new engine for the same vehicle. I asked him, "We just put a new transmission in, why do we need a new engine?" He replied, "The vehicle won't go over 10 miles per hour. It's just underpowered." I asked him again, "Did you use the manual?" This time he got a little mad, "You're always questioning my integrity." We tracked down a new engine.

A few days later he walks into my office a third time, "We need a new transmission." I had had about enough. I asked, "Why? We gave you a new transmission a week ago, and we gave you a new engine to boot. I'll bet there is something else wrong." He got this really arrogant look in his eye and developed a little sheepish smile, "If you think you can do better, by all means show me."

I grabbed my coveralls, a manual, and walked out to the vehicle and

---

52. The FIST-V is a tracked vehicle used by fire support—it sits on an M113 chassis. It stands for FIre SupporT-Vehicle.

said, "If I can figure this out in less than ten minutes you and your whole section owe me 1,000 push-ups. If not, I'll owe you 1,000. Deal?" He shook my hand and I went to work.

The second step in the troubleshooting manual for a track with an "underpowered" issue is to check the linkage between the engine and transmission. I crawled my butt into the engine compartment and noticed the bolts connecting the linkage were not only backwards, they were too long and it was catching on the engine oil pan. I crawled out, grabbed a couple of wrenches, then walked over to the bolt bin and picked out the correct sized bolts. I then crawled back inside the engine compartment and put it together correctly—all within the span of about eight minutes.

During the test drive, the vehicle was purring at about 25-30 miles per hour. I looked at the NCO and said, "That's why we have manuals... now push."

THE FIELD PROBLEM FROM HELL... AND THE CAT

IT MUST HAVE BEEN AROUND NOVEMBER 2002 WHEN THE BATTALION headed to the field for the first time since my arrival. We had already gone through the whole maintenance debacle and the battalion was looking pretty good for the most part. But, as any old maintenance tech or motor sergeant will tell you, as soon as you roll out the gate you will really find out your true maintenance posture. It is to be expected that the first couple of days the gremlins will come out but eventually all the kinks get worked out and everything will eventually smooth out as far as maintenance is concerned.

The spring, summer, and fall of 2002 must have been one of the driest in the record books. I think the last time it rained must have been February of that year. However, the day after my battalion rolled to the field the heavens opened up and the rains poured. I don't think it stopped the entire three weeks we were in the field. Maneuvering pretty much came to a standstill. It was the running joke that if Texas ever wanted to end a drought all they had to do was send us to the field. For some reason, it seems that God likes it to rain on soldiers in the field. Not that I'm complaining, I mean I am sure all those farmers out there really loved it! It just makes for a miserable time in the field. But, a soldier's life is to embrace the miserable and excel.

We set the Unit Maintenance Collection Point on top of a hill so the water wouldn't pool around our area and mostly drain away. The UMCP is the place all the broken vehicles are collected, triaged, and then repaired—kinda like a hospital for vehicles. Chief and I would drive around together in a vain effort to help the recovery teams pull vehicles out of the mud. I'm not sure there was really anything we could have done, but sitting around idle isn't in my blood so we did what we could.

One painstaking sight I remember was watching a recovery crew try to pull a broken down howitzer across a field. The field was almost a swamp by now. The recovery vehicle crew pulled that vehicle as far as they could until the recovery vehicle became bogged down in the mud. Then, the crew disconnected from the howitzer and pulled about a hundred feet or so in front of the downed howitzer and paid out their main winch (my thoughts retuned to an earlier experience of a main winch snapping...) I was concerned after my earlier experiences doing something similar. However, I had faith that my crews were better trained so I watched from a distance. I was proud of that crew as I watch them expertly pull that howitzer across that field using their main winch without incident. It was a slow process but it had to be done. Eventually, they made it all the way across the field, tied onto the howitzer again and motored away to the UMCP.

Enter the cat. My wife had been on me about getting the kids a cat for months. I had been dragging my feet because (now don't hate me) I have never been a cat lover. Truth is, I don't like to have to work for affection from my animals. But, sitting on top of this hill next to the UMCP, there was this stray cat that picked me out of the group to hang around. I didn't feed her. I didn't pet her. I didn't even pay any attention to her—at first. Every night, as I pulled out my cot and sleeping bag, somehow she would find some way to work herself into my shelter and crawl on top of my feet. I even shooed her away a couple of times. But she was persistent.

After a couple of days of this I called my wife and asked her to meet me on one of the range roads. I had a surprise. My wife showed up and I handed her the cat. She took the cat to the vet and made sure she was healthy, got all her shots, and was de-wormed. The vet guessed her age at about ten months or so but said it was really hard to tell. As of the writing of this book I still have the cat and she looks exactly the same. She must be an eternal cat.

THE FIST-V

NOW, LET ME EXPLAIN A LITTLE MORE ABOUT A FIST-V. IT HAS ALL THE necessary equipment on board to assist an artillerist to rain death and destruction down on the enemy. Again, it is based on a M113 family of vehicles which, if you remember, I am intimately familiar with and although relatively simple, some of the repairs can be a real pain.

Towards the end of the field exercise from hell, one of the FIST-Vs had a piece of the transmission linkage snap. It was the part that attaches inside the transmission so it's not a really easy fix. A transmission swap is in order. Only problem was, we didn't have any transmissions on hand and it would take about three weeks to get one it. We had used up our quota of transmissions in an earlier story…

Anyway, the solution we came up with was to weld the piece back onto the transmission as a quick fix in order to get the vehicle back into the fight. Then we would order a transmission and replace it as soon as it arrived. The welded piece held up for the remainder of the field exercise.

When we returned from the field and finally received the transmission, I called the officer in charge of the vehicle so as to schedule a time when we could replace the transmission. He more or less refused. He said the vehicle worked fine and he didn't see the point of repairing a vehicle that was operational. Normally I would agree with him, however, in this case it was only a matter of time before that weld broke and the vehicle would need repair anyway.

He and I went back and forth on the subject until finally, as we couldn't agree, the matter went to the battalion commander. He made his argument and I made mine. I guess he made a better argument 'cause the commander told me to mothball the transmission and leave the subject alone. I tried to appeal by saying, "Typically, the part will break at the worst possible moment and I hope no one gets hurt because of it."

My appeal ultimately failed but, my prediction held true. The little piece on the transmission decided to break as the vehicle was being moved from a port in Kuwait to Camp Pennsylvania, our staging point for the invasion of Iraq. But, that's another story…

EPILOGUE

THE REST OF THE STORY

THE FIST-V HAD BROKEN DOWN AT THE WORST POSSIBLE MOMENT. WE had brought an extra transmission. I knew exactly where it was. Problem was, I couldn't get to it. The transmission was in a CONEX sitting on a boat in the middle of Kuwait Bay. The battalion commander was pretty ticked. I think he was madder at himself than he was at me because he had not listened to Chief and me earlier; but the situation remained. I assured him that as soon as the CONEX made it off the boat we would track down the transmission and have it replaced.

But that wasn't good enough. There are vehicles that are dragged around by our support unit known as ORFs (Operational Readiness Floats–pronounced like its spelled). These are vehicles that are in place and supposed to be utilized in the event of a vehicle being destroyed or rendered inoperable due to enemy action. The FIST officer and I again made our arguments to the commander. Again I lost the argument (I must really suck at arguing…). The commander made the decision to "Float the ORF."

Floating the ORF isn't all that easy. Although it is the same vehicle, it doesn't have all the operational equipment on board—things like radios, antennas, computer systems, etc. It takes about twenty-four hours of continuous work to upgrade an ORF to functional. After the decision was made to "Float the ORF", about three hours later the transmission was located and about two hours after that the transmission was replaced and the vehicle was fully operational. It took another day and a half to finish floating the ORF. If only the commander had some tactical patience that team would have been in the fight sooner rather than later. The decision wasn't mine but the results were my fault I suppose. I just happened to be paper the shit had stuck to. I never did really respect that FIST officer after that and I lost a little respect for the commander as well.

By the way, all that maintenance pain we had gone through about eight months earlier paid off big time. Other than the FIST-V right off the boat, we didn't have another vehicle break down until about fifty miles south of Baghdad. The other units in the brigade? They were strung out up and down the road over the entire six hundred miles between Kuwait and Baghdad. Something I am rather proud of.

CHIEF, ME, AND THE RANGE

I WANTED TO PAY TRIBUTE TO A MAN I USED TO TRULY RESPECT. DEPLOY-ments, war, and recovering from these hardships can take a toll on a person. Some folks never recover and just continue to suffer. Too proud to ask or receive help, and too stubborn to accept it—yet in need of it all the same. The man I'm talking about was the warrant officer who was with me during my first deployment. To put it bluntly, about two months before we deployed he received some devastating news. He had Multiple Sclerosis.

As soon as we received deployment orders, one of his doctors deemed him as "non-deployable." Now Chief, being of warrior stock, fought this tooth and nail. He went so far as to tell the battalion commander, "If you leave me behind I'll meet you in Kuwait"– meaning, he'd buy his own plane ticket. You have to love a guy like that.

Anyway, the only reason the doctor didn't want him to go had to do with the lack of availability of the medication prescribed to treat the illness. The doctor said it had to be refrigerated, which ultimately turned out to not be true. Nonetheless here we are. So we devised a rig and outfitted it with a refrigerator and a generator with enough energy production to maintain proper coolness. Problem solved.

The next problem he faced was qualification with his weapon. Now, normally that would not have been a problem. Chief can shoot fairly well. However, for those not in the know, one of his symptoms associated with his illness is sometimes he loses sight in his right eye. As he is right handed, this can be a problem during weapon qualification. So, how did I help my buddy out?

During his time in the foxhole at the range, I occupied the one next to him. After the range was open and we commenced firing, I shot his targets instead of mine. After I had used up all my rounds (I still had to qualify myself...), I pulled out some binoculars and lay down next to him.

"Shoot," I said.

"Ray, I can't see the target!"

"Don't worry about it, shoot!" He squeezed the trigger and I saw the impact.

"Aim a little to the left!" He shot again.

"A little more!" This time he hit the target.

"Hit it again!" He plugged three more rounds into that target.

I adjusted him onto enough targets so he could qualify. I know I cheated a little. But, when a buddy is down you help him out!

GLOSSARY OF ACRONYMS AND TERMS

#'S

1LT—First Lieutenant. The second rank within the officers rank structure. The rank is a single silver bar. The first lieutenant is supposed to be the most experienced lieutenant. The name of the rank is a throwback to Napoleonic armies when soldiers would line up in ranks, march within about a hundred feet of each other, aim, then shoot at each other. The first lieutenant would stand on the far left hand side of the first rank of soldiers.

1SG—First Sergeant. Today this is used to describe the senior NCO of a company sized element. The name of the rank is a throwback to Napoleonic armies when soldiers would line up in ranks, march within about a hundred feet of each other, aim, then shoot at each other. The first sergeant would stand on the far right hand side of the first rank of soldiers. In the second rank was the second sergeant… you get the idea.

2LT—Second Lieutenant. The first rank within the officers rank structure. The rank is a single gold bar—also known as a "Butter Bar" cause it looks like a bar of butter. The second lieutenant is not expected to have much experience. As noted above, the second lieutenant would stand at the far left of the second rank of soldiers in the Napoleonic armies.

A

AAFES—Army and Air Force Exchange Service. See PX.

ACU—Army Combat Uniform. The uniform that succeeded the BDU uniform (Late 1980's to Mid 2000's). The ACU is a light green on lighter green digital pattern uniform worn during and after the Iraq and Afghan wars.

ADC-S—Assistant Division Commander—Supply or Logistics. The

ADC-S is generally a one star general and is responsible for all logistics within a division.

ADC-M—Assistant Division Commander—Maneuver. The ADC-M is generally a one star general and is responsible for all coordination of resources as it pertains to training and movement of the division.

AFN- Armed Forces Network. The army controlled radio and television stations while overseas in Europe, Asia, etc. It's "not for profit" broadcasting for US soldiers. Also a good way for the senior leadership to put general information out to soldiers in the field.

AIT—Advanced Individual Training. The army training where a soldier receives his/her elected MOS training. For example, I was a tracked vehicle repairman and all tracked vehicle repairman would receive training at Aberdeen Proving Grounds, Edgewood Arsenal, Maryland.

ALO—Army Liaison Officer. When two units are assigned to work together they generally exchange one officer and one NCO to act as liaisons.

APFT—Army Physical Fitness Test. The test a soldier has to pass in order to be eligible for promotion and retention in the army. The APFT consists of three timed events. Push-ups, sit-ups, and a two mile run. A soldier must score at least 60 points in each event with a minimum overall score of 180. The minimum standard for scoring the points depends on the soldier's age. A soldier who scores the minimum is generally not considered a good soldier.

ARTEP—ARmy Training and Evaluation Program. An event where a larger unit, generally a battalion size or larger, goes through a series of events simulating their unique role in a wartime environment. For example, an Infantry unit might conduct a "Movement to Contact" where as a Military Intelligence unit might conduct surveillance over the radio waves during the same training event.

AWOL—Absent WithOut Leave. When a soldier leaves a unit without permission for more than 24 hours. Less than 24 hours the soldier is considered "Out of Ranks" or "Unaccounted for" meaning "We're still looking for him."

B

Battery—The company sized element when referencing an Artillery unit or an Air Defense Artillery Unit. The term "battery" goes all the way back to before Roman times. When one army wanted to "batter" down the walls or the gate where the other army was hiding they would call upon specialized soldiers to build battering rams also known as batteries. During the dawn of the artillery age, the original cannons or howitzers were used to replace the battering ram. Apparently, flinging a projectile at a gate at subsonic speeds from a distance puts these specialized in less danger. Eventually, generals discovered the artillery pieces could be used to mow down other armies at a greater distance as well. The birth of the artillery.

BC—Battery Commander—or—Battalion Commander depending on the context.

Battery Commander—The commander of an Artillery or Air Defense Artillery company sized element (generally between 50 and 150 soldiers).

Battalion Commander—The commander of most battalion sized units in the army (generally 300—1000 soldiers).

BDU—Battle Dress Uniform. A woodland camouflaged uniform worn by soldiers from the late 1980's through the mid 2000's. They succeeded the fatigue uniform (olive green 100% cotton) and preceded the ACU (Army Combat Uniform).

BMO—Battery Maintenance Officer—or—Battalion Maintenance Officer depending on the context.

Battery Maintenance Officer. An additional duty assigning a lieutenant at the battery level the responsibility over the maintenance section.

Battalion Maintenance Officer. The primary duty of all maintenance responsibilities given to a less experience Captain on a battalion staff.

BMS—Battalion Maintenance Sergeant—The NCO in charge of a Battalion level maintenance facility.

BMT—Battalion Maintenance Technician. An expert on all maintenance related actives. A technician in the army is a warrant officer. The warrant officer is a special breed of soldier who dedicates his career to his/her given field of expertise. A warrant officer's rank falls somewhere between an NCO and an Officer.

BOC—Battery Operations Center. In the field, the operations center is where all planning and coordination is made in an artillery battery.

BOSS—Better Opportunity for Single Soldiers. An army program designed to provide a better overall experience for single soldiers in the army. If the army had unions this would be a union for single soldiers.

BRM—Basic Rifleman Marksmanship. The term given to the training the army does associated with shooting rifles.

C

CDR—Commander. Abbreviation used for a commander at any level.

CID—Criminal Investigation Division. The military police version of a warrant officer. They are basically Internal Affairs investigators in the army. They investigate army crimes like murder, rape, etc.

CIF—Central Issue Facility. A centralized place on most larger army posts responsible for issuing army field training gear. Gear like, helmets, sleeping bags, etc. The gear is also known as "TA-50" or "table of allowances 50"—individual gear. A Soldier will often refer to this equipment as "TA-50" or "CIF." Before heading to the field a platoon sergeant will often inspect his platoon's TA-50 or CIF for accountability.

Company—The term used to descried a unit of soldiers of between 50-150. A company is a throwback to older times when a wealthy individual would organize a local militia and provide all equipment the unit needed, the wealthy man would generally be known as the "company commander" since he paid for everything and therefore owned everything. The other officers would then be elected into position.

Company Grade Officers—The term used to describe the officer generally associated with a Company, Battery, or Troop. The ranks are 2LT, 1LT, and CPT.

COL—Colonel. The sixth rank within the officers rank structure. The rank is a single silver eagle also known as "full bird colonel." The Colonel is the senior rank amongst the field grade officers.

CPT—Captain. The third rank within the officers rank structure. The rank is two silver bars. Also known as "railroad tracks" because they resemble a set of tracks. The captain is supposed to be the most experienced amongst the company grade officers.

CQ—Charge of Quarters. The CQ is generally a junior NCO and a lower enlisted soldier who act as the responsible parties at night while the commander is away. If there is an altercation or a violation of policy the CQ is supposed to control the situation and report to the commander in the morning. If the issue has immediacy the CQ is supposed to call the commander and inform.

CSM—Command Sergeant Major. The command sergeant major is the highest enlist soldier in units above a company (battalion, brigade, etc). The command sergeant major is supposed to act as the soldiers representative to the commander. There are some soldier issues a commander may not fully understand and command sergeant major brings a "soldiers sense" to the situation. The term sergeant major is a throwback to yester years when the Majors would run the field issuing orders to the companies. From time to time the battalion commander would need an additional field runner and the sergeant major would fill that roll.

CTLT—CadeT LieutenanT. A CTLT is an officer in training temporarily assigned to active duty for the purposes of gaining experience.

D

DPW—Department of Public Works. Civilians contracted by the army to perform maintenance of buildings and other facilities.

E

ETS—End Term of Service. Date when a soldier is supposed to get out of the army.

F

FBCB²—Force twenty one Battle Command Brigade and Below. Known as FBCB two. An army tactical navigation and communication system that was the precursor to the global positioning system.

FDC—Fire Direction Center. Located in an operations center, the FDC is where ballistic data is computed for the firing of artillery projectiles.

Field Grade Officers—The term used to describe the officer generally associated with a battalion or brigade. The ranks are MAJ, LTC, and COL. Field grade is a throwback term associated with the officers responsible for "running the field" and issuing orders to subordinate units in days gone by.

FIST-V—FIre SupporT Vehicle. The FIST-V is a tracked vehicle used by fire support—it sits on an M113 chassis.

FM—Field Manuals. Manuals written by the army to tell the soldier how to do everything the army has to do. Generally speaking, the manuals describe terms as set "in a perfect world" and around guidelines rather than hard and fast rules.

FO—Forward Observer. The lowest echelon in the world of Fire Support. The individual who initiates the call for indirect fires.

FOB—Forward Operating Base. Basically a place where we made our home while deployed in Iraq or Afghanistan.

FRG—Family Readiness Group. A group normally made up of spouses and generally lead by one of the more senior spouses

FTX—Field Training Exercise. Training conducted out in the training areas away from normal mainstream post life.

G

GEN—General Officer. There are five general officer ranks. The progressive ranks start with Brigadier General, then Major General, Lieutenant General, General, and General of the Armies. Each progression is associated with more stars, hence one star, two stars, etc. The rank of five stars hasn't been used since GEN Bradley died in the late 1970's and will probably never be used again. It is more of an honorary rank rather than a true rank. My understanding of the general officer ranks is, they give up their associated branch and become "general officers" meaning they can assume any posting required.

Go-fering—Country boy term used for a fella who "go's fer this or that.'

GPS—Global Positioning System. If you don't know what this is then, well, climb out of your hole.

GPV—General Purpose Vehicle. The original "Jeep" you know, GP (phonetically pronounced "jeep')

H

HEMAT—Heavy Expanded Mobility Ammunition Trailer. The trailer for the HEMTT.

HEMTT—Heavy Expanded Mobility Tactical Truck. A really big truck used to haul cargo around the battle field.

HHB—Headquarters, Headquarters Battery.—The main battery in an artillery battalion used to support the staff of that battalion.

HMMWV—Highly Mobile Multipurpose Wheeled Vehicle. Also

known as a "Hummer." It is the main "gettin' around" vehicle used by the army.

I

IA—Internal Affairs. If you've seen "Law and Order" on TV then you know what Internal Affairs is. If not, crawl out of your house and get a life.

IG—Inspector General. The organization in the army who works directly for the commanding general and is charged with enforcing army policies through inspections.

K

KP—Kitchen Patrol. Augmentee to for army cooks to abuse.

L

LT—Lieutenant. A general term used to describe any lieutenant.

LTC—Lieutenant Colonel. The fifth rank within the officers rank structure. The rank is a single silver oak leaf also known as "light colonel." The LTC is the middle rank amongst the field grade officers.

M

M2 Machinegun—Also known as the "Ma Deuce." A browning fully automatic .50 calibur machinegun first introduced in World War I as a antiaircraft gun. Over the past hundred or so years it remains relative unchanged. It is very accurate and powerful.

M3A1 Machinegun—Also known as the "Grease Gun" because it looks like a grease tube with a barrel welded on one end. It's a .45 caliber fully automatic submachine gun which is relatively impossible to aim or hit anything aimed at. It's kick is tremendous and its barrel is short meaning, it ain't very accurate. If anyone tells you they can shoot this thing and actually hit anything, they're probably lying.

MAJ—Major. The four rank within the officers rank structure. The rank is a single gold oak leaf. The Major is the junior rank amongst the field grade officers. It is also the rank I achieved prior to my retirement. My father would describe the rank of major as being the hardest rank in the army. Captains don't listen to you and Colonel's ignore you.

MDMP—Military Decision Making Process. This is a process whereas the army super analyzes any given mission looking for the best course of action in order to accomplish the mission.

MEPS—Military Entrance Processing Station. The place where most enlisted folks go to process into the army. Generally speaking the new soldier is given a physical and there is lots of paperwork. As a side note, my grandfather used to say, half of the doctors out there graduated at the bottom of their class. Well, I believe those doctors found employment at MEPS...

MI—Military Inteligence. A branch in the army. Also, sometimes a contradiction in terms, however, the military intelligence isn't the mainstream definition. It means to learn about your enemy and analysis a way to defeat him.

MILES Gear—Multiple Integrated Laser Engagement System Gear. Essentially the precursor to laser tag. Really bulky and often not working.

MILKY—I really don't know what this acronym means. I have checked with several of my buddies from those days and they are clueless too. If you happen to know let me know and I'll buy you a beer. Until then, it's a really sophisticated piece of machinery used for either jamming or listening to enemy radio broadcasts.

MLRS—Multiple Launch Rocket System. A really cool vehicle used to shoot rockets a really long distances and blows a lot of stuff up.

MOPP—Mission Oriented Protective Posture. Term given to the gear designed to allow a soldier the ability to function in a contaminated environment for up to six hours. It is broken down into different levels.

MOPP level 0—Gear is clean and available.

MOPP level 1—Pants and Jacket are worn.

MOPP level 2—Pants, Jacket, and boots are worn.

MOPP level 3—Pants, Jacket, boots, and mask are worn

MOPP level 4—Pants, Jacket, boots, gloves, and mask is worn. If you find yourself in this configuration I hope you're training because otherwise...you're fucked.

MOS—Military Occupation Specialty. The job a soldier has signed up to perform. Example, an 11B in your basic infantryman. A 92Y is a logistic clerk. Etc. The numbering is changed constantly so by the time this book is published those descriptions will be wrong.

MP—Military Police. A branch in the army. They're police need I say more?

MRE—Meal Ready to Eat. A brown or tan bagged meal that is rumored to last decades is kept in a stable environment. Also known as "Mr. E's" or Mysteries cause there's really no telling what's in there. Truthfully, the meals have improved tremendously over the years. Most are actually pretty good.

MS—Military Science. The minor degree an officer receives while attending ROTC in college. Also associated with the ranking of cadets in college.

MS1—Freshman

MS2—Sophomore

MS3—Junior

MS4—Senior

MTOE—Modified Table of Organization and Equipment. A table produced by echelons above reality and approved by congress, it tells a commander how he is supposed to organize his unit and what equipment he should have. Often times a commander understands but doesn't follow this guidance. It's understood a commander should have the ability to organize however he needs to accomplish the mission.

N

NATO—North Atlantic Treaty Organization. If you don't know what this is, head back to high school social studies…

NBC—Nuclear, Biological, and Chemical. Very bad. Also known as "weapons of mass destruction." Believe it or not, a soldier is expected to finish the mission regardless of the NBC environment…Hence the MOPP gear.

NCO—Non-Commissioned Officer. The more senior of the enlisted ranks. NCO ranks run from Sergeant through Command Sergeant Major. Most of these folks are really good at what they do. The officer issues the instructions and the NCOs execute the mission under the supervision of the officer. NCOs execute and Officer resource.

NCOER—Non-Commissioned Officer Evaluation Report. The NCOs annual report card.

NCOIC—Non-Commissioned Officer In Charge. The top NCO of any given Mission.

Needling—Country boy term for poking fun at a fella just for laughs. This practice sometimes ends with broken noses or blacked eyes. Yet, it can still be fun...

NMSU—New Mexico State University. A rather good college located in Las Cruces, New Mexico. At the time of the writing of this book there was an ROTC department at this college.

O

OBC—Officer Basic Course. Where a 2LT goes to learn how to be a 2LT...

OER—Officer Evaluation Report. The annual report card for an officer.

OIC—Officer In Charge. The head officer in charge of a given mission.

OPD—Officer Professional Development. Where officers gather around a given location and are offered classes on professional subjects. Often there is a guest speaker or a history lesson of some kind.

OPFOR—OPposing FORces. Soldiers who, often donning enemy outfits, play the "bad guys" during FTXs

ORF—Operational Readiness Float. A vehicle set aside and maintained just in case one of the essential vehicles is damaged or destroyed. The float is a replacement vehicle.

P

PA—Physician's Assistant. Look this one up on your own if you don't know what it is...

PAC—Personnel Actions Center. Also known as the S1 Shop. This is the section where personnel administration actions are staff and tracked. Things like evaluation reports, awards, and pay.

PCS—Permanent Change of Station. When a Soldier moves from one unit to another. Most often associated with a move to a different post.

PFC—Private First Class. The third rank within the enlisted rank structure. The rank is a single chevron with a single rocker. The PFC is the senior rank amongst the privates in the army.

PL—Platoon Leader. Often a Lieutenant. A platoon is the lowest unit an officer is assigned to. There are more than one platoons in a company.

PVT—Private. The PVT is the lowest rank in the army. Private is a throwback rank which used to be associated with volunteers or those "pressed into service." Yes, way back in the day when the king came calling you either volunteered or they forced you to fight. These folks were known as "Private" soldiers or "Private Citizen" soldiers meaning they weren't regular army.

PMS—Professor of Military Science. The senior officer in charge of an ROTC detachement.

POC—Platoon Operations Center. In the artillery, a Platoon has an operations center as well, mostly this is for FDC functions, but this location is often used for planning as well.

PSG—Platoon Sergeant. The PSG is the senior NCO of a Platoon.

PT—Physical Training. The most sacred time in the army. At least once a day for at least an hour the soldier is supposed to do some sort of physical activity. While in garrison, the time allotted is from 0630 to 0730 (6:30 am ot 7:30 am for you civilians).

PV2—Private Two. The second rank within the enlist rank structure. The rank is a single chevron also known as "mosquito wings." The PV2 is the middle rank amongst privates.

PX—Post Exchange. Also known as AAFES. A general store on post. The PX also follows soldiers all over the world. Their motto is, where there's soldiers AAFES will be there. A place kinda like a Wal-Mart. In Iraq or Afghanistan, on the most remote of FOBs, there was at least a small shop where, when supplied, a soldier could buy sundry goods and some candy.

Q

QA/QC—Quality Assurance/Quality Control. I think that is rather self explanatory.

R

(R)—Retired. When you see this behind someone's rank it means they have retired.

ROTC—Reserved Officer Training Corps. Where about 80% of the officers earn their commissions while at college. Most larger colleges have an ROTC programs.

RP—Rally Point—or- Release point depending on the context.

Rally Point—A place designated to meet if all else goes to hell.

Release Point—A point where a movement has been concluded. At this point the maneuvering unit is released to do what it needs to do.

S

SGM—Sergeant Major. A staff version of a Command Sergeant Major. See CSM.

SGT—Sergeant. The fifth rank within the enlisted rank structure. The rank is three chevrons also known as "buck sergeant." The sergeant is the junior rank amongst the non-commissioned officers. The word "sergeant" is used when talking to any of the NCOs with the exception of the First Sergeant and the Sergeant Major.

SMK—Smoke. Abbreviation used to describe that white cloudy stuff produced when there is a fire. Also, in the artillery, SMK is used as a substitute for PSG. It stands for "Chief of Smoke" meaning, he is the most experienced NCO in the platoon.

SP—Start Point. The point where a unit starts a movement.

SPC—Specialist. A Specialist is a unique rank. More experienced than a PVT or PFC yet not quite an NCO. Sometimes referred to as a "Junior NCO" but that doesn't really explain it. Typically, a SPC is the only guy in the unit who really knows what is going on and is not afraid to tell you about it. The PVTs are scared and the NCOs are too professional. Back in the day, there was a whole slew of specialist ranks (SP4—SP7). These used to be the feeder ranks for the warrant officers. Sometime in the 1980's the army did away with the specialist ranks with the exception of the SP4 which is now SPC.

SSG—Staff Sergeant. The rank is three chevron's with one rocker. One rank higher than a buck sergeant.

STX Lanes—Situational Training eXercise Lanes. A sequential set of situational events along a lane. Generally, a unit (generally a smaller unit 4—10 folks) is given a set of grid coordinates on a map and it has to navigate to the start point of the lane. Once at the start point a TAC issues the unit its mission and the leader has to plan, coordinate, and issue instructions to the rest of the unit. The unit navigates the lane and has to react to whatever situation which occurs. The intent is to provide a "near real life" or "combat" situation without actually putting anyone in a life threaten situation.

T

TAC—Tactical Officer—or—Tactical NCO. A TAC is a trainer when an individual or unit is in a training environment. The TAC is supposed to be a subject matter expert and most times acts as an Observer / Controller (OC) with the intent to keep the training event on track for its intended purpose and to keep it from spiraling out of control if something unexpected occurs.

TC—Training Circular—or—Truck Commander—or—Track Commander—or—Troop Commander depending on the context implied during the conversation.

Training Circular—A brochure which offers training and generally focuses on a singular topic.

Truck Commander—The individual who sits in the front right hand seat of a vehicle and is in control of the vehicle. The TC is generally the highest ranking individual in the vehicle. The TC navigates and tells the driver where to turn, how fast to drive, when to stop. A good driver does exactly what the TC says. If the vehicle where to get caught speeding or some other illicit activity, the TC assumes all responsibility.

Track Commander—Just like above except the Track Commander generally sits in the highest cupola of the tracked vehicle.

Troop Commander—The commander of a company sized element within a Calvary Squadron. A through back to the days of horse backed calvary.

TFT—Tabular Firing Table. The TFT is also known as the "Big Brown Hinky"—I have no idea where that name came from; it just is. Its is a huge manual where a fire direction officer or NCO goes to find the data to compute ballistic data.

TM—Technical Manual. A manual where a soldier goes to find out everything about a piece of equipment. It is basically an owner's manual for army equipment.

TMP—Transpiration Motor Pool. A place where one goes to borrow a common vehicle, if authorized.

TTP's—Tactics, Techniques, and Procedures. Basically a "how to" list for accomplishing the more difficult actions in the army. For example, while working in an operations center, when an attack happens there should be a list of TTP's on who to call, what to do, and what is important. These are changed from time to time based on different circumstances.

TWOT—Training WithtOut Troops. Pronounced Twoot. When a Staff needs to conduct training but there isn't a need to actually maneuver troops out in the field. A very cost effective way to train.

U

UCMJ—Uniformed Code of Military Justice. The military's justice system. I'm not a lawyer but, it is a set of rules that are relatively unbreakable, or if you break one it is generally a federal offence and there is a jail term associated with it. For example, Article 134, the General Article, also known as the catch all, basically says that anything a soldier does that the commander can deem as "contrary to good discipline for the unit" is punishable. So, violate at your own risk. Though it can happen most often it doesn't. Most commanders were knuckleheads at one point in their own lives and understand.

UMCP—Unit Maintenance Collection Point. The place where the unit drags it's broken vehicle's while in the field. An orgy of fixing broken vehicle's.

X

XO—Executive Officer. The second in command as any given unit company or higher. He is generally responsible for all logistics.

AFTERWORD

I THINK THIS IS A GOOD PLACE TO FINISH THIS BOOK. THERE'S A LOT MORE to my story, and I'll complete it soon. Like all good stories, mine needs to ferment in my melon for a while longer. I hope the reader has thoroughly enjoyed this book and my view of knuckleheads. Upon reflection of my life—and I think my father would agree—I'm probably the biggest knucklehead of them all.

Truthfully we all have the propensity to act in a knuckleheaded way. Always remember, there's a guy like me watching from around the corner thinking, *Good Lord, what a knucklehead.*

ABOUT THE AUTHOR

RAYMOND JONES IS A TWENTY-FIVE YEAR COMBAT VETERAN OF THE UNITed States Army. He has deployed five times, including three tours to Iraq and two to Afghanistan. His combat tours to Iraq include time as Maintenance Officer, a Battalion Fire Support Officer, and an Operations Battle Major on a Brigade Staff. His combat tours to Afghanistan include time as Mobile Training Team Leader and an Artillery Subject Matter Expert on a corps level staff. He entered his military service as a private in 1989 in the Texas Army National Guard, transferred to active duty in 1991 with a tour to Germany (1991-1994) and a tour at Fort Carson Colorado (1995). He transferred back into the Texas Army National Guard while he attended ROTC at Tarleton State University where he earned his Bachelor's Degree in Economics before returning to Active Duty as a Field Artillery officer at Fort Sill Oklahoma (1998-2002). Later he transferred to Fort Hood Texas where his deploy cycle began until his retirement in 2014. Raymond Jones still lives in Central Texas, near Fort Hood, with his wife, Dallice.

HIS COMBAT RESUME INCLUDES:

March-July 2003—Battalion Maintenance Officer 4-42 FA

July 2003-March 2004—Fire Support Officer 1-22 IN

December 2005-August 2006—Battery Commander B/2-77 FA

August 2006-Dec 2006—Squadron Fire Support Officer 8/10 CAV

July 2008-April 2009—Brigade Operations Battle Major 41st Fires Brigade

September 2011-June 2012—Mobile Training Team Leader- RMTC-E Afghanistan

April -August 2013—SME Artillery, IJC, Kabul, Afghanistan

HIS AWARDS INCLUDE:

Bronze Star Medal 2nd oak leaf cluster (three awards)

Meritorious Service Medal 1st oak leaf cluster (two awards)

Army Commendation Medal 3rd oak leaf cluster (four awards)

Army Achievement Medal 5th oak leaf cluster (six awards)

Valorous Unit Award

Meritorious Unit Citation

National Defense Service Medal

Afghan Campaign Medal

Iraqi Campaign Medal

Global War on Terrorism Expeditionary Medal

Global War of Terrorism Service Medal

NATO Medal

EXCERPT FROM:

WE WERE KNUCKLEHEADS ONCE... AND ALWAYS

DEPLOYMENT TO IRAQ

IN JANUARY 2003, WE LOADED ALL OUR VEHICLES ON A BOAT IN THE GULF of Mexico and headed to Iraq. We were supposed to land in Turkey then drive six hundred miles to a staging area. A staging area is a place where we'd build what's called "combat power," meaning we'd assemble and process troops and equipment. Instead we landed in Kuwait behind the 101st Airborne Division and began to build combat power in Kuwait. We were there for about nineteen days before we made the mad rush north. That was one of the longest convoys I've ever been on.

I was the convoy leader for most of the ash and trash[53] because I had what's known as FBCB2.[54] I had graphics on my digital map (graphics are the way armies move on the battlefield; they offer routes and checkpoints for what we call "battle tracking"), but about thirty minutes prior to SP (Start Point or Start Patrol)[55], my FBCB2[56] took a dirt nap. It completely shut down and wouldn't start back up.

I quickly jumped out of my vehicle, grabbed a handful of markers and an MRE (Meals Ready to Eat)[57] box cover and began to copy the map and graphics from an FBCB2 that was in the vehicle next to mine. You may be asking, "Why didn't he just use a map?" Truthfully there weren't any maps. The big he-man general in charge had said, "We're the digital

---

53. Ash and trash is a common reference to logistics. You know, supply, maintenance, and other stuff.
54. The FBCB2 stands for "Force XXI (21) Battle Command Brigade and Below." It's the army version of a Garmin, except the army version is a lot bigger. It is maybe four or five cubic feet, a lot heavier—maybe fifteen pounds, and consisted of five separate components.—In a nutshell, it is a piece of junk.
55. To SP army speak for "Go!" or "I'm Going NOW!"
56. FBCB2 is the precursor to GPS navigation. It's a really big computer that tracks where vehicles are on a digital map. It also allows the user to see other units or vehicles in the general vicinity.
57. The MRE is supposed to provide all the calories and nutrients a going boy (or girl) needs to survive. Often referred to as "Mr. E's" or "Mysteries" because you never know what you're going to get.

division. We don't use maps." Great, until your FBCB2 craps out. At any rate, I copied as much as I could.

SP time came, and we all began the rush north along the Iraqi Highway 1, which fortunately was the only highway headed north into Iraq. Also, fortunately, it appeared all the coalition vehicles were headed to the same location—namely Baghdad. I "faked the funk"[58] as the convoy leader, but in reality I just followed the convoy in front of me. That was until the second day.

You see, along the route there were checkpoints and fuel points. At the fuel point we were directed to the vehicle top-off area then corralled into an area and left there for a few hours. The intention was for us to rest a bit, eat a bit, and use the facilities. At my second or third fuel point, we were directed to the holding area, and I told my driver to take a little nap, and I'd wake him up when it was time to go. The next thing I remember was waking up to find that the convoy I'd been following was gone. I panicked a little on the inside but quickly pulled myself together, jumped out of my vehicle, and ran down my convoy line, waking all the truck and track commanders and instructing them to wake the drivers and get ready to go.

The way I figured it, Kuwait was south and Baghdad was north. I pulled out my handy-dandy compass and said in my best command voice, "Turn right." I didn't have any checkpoints on my hand-drawn map, and even if I did, I didn't have any grid coordinates or reference points. I was essentially driving blind into Iraq. Eventually we came to a Y in the road. I looked up at the road signs and saw squiggles and an arrow pointing left with a big "1" in a white square and a bunch of squiggles and an arrow pointing right with a big "1" in a white square. Uh-oh.

Images flashed through my brain. I kept envisioning newsreels of the 507th Maintenance Company ambushed in the battle of Nasiriyah. Again I pulled out my compass then said in my most confident voice, "This road is more north. Go right." I kept thinking, *My pistol ain't got no bullets, but maybe I can throw it at the bad guys.* My platoon sergeant had forgotten that I had a 9mm instead of a rifle. He didn't draw any pistol bullets, just rifle bullets. When I tracked down the supply sergeant, he told me the battery commander had all the 9mm bullets. Try as I might,

---

58. To "Fake the Funk" is also known as "Dick Dancing" meaning "I didn't know what the hell I'm doing but I'm going put on airs as if I did." Basically, when a leader gets all confused and twisted around sometimes it is better to "fake the funk" rather than let your subordinates know just how fucked up you really are...)

I never could find the battery commander. One thing you never miss in the army is SP time. I'd rather face a horde of angry Iraqis than face my battalion commander after I'd missed SP.

We rolled through Baghdad on what turned into "Route Irish." I kept the convoy on a mostly northern route, as I knew my battalion had to be around there somewhere. The houses began to thin out a little, and then I saw the most beautiful sight—a HMMWV with my battalion's bumper number on it. It was parked off to the side with a couple of soldiers pulling guard. I pulled up and said, "Where's the rest of the battalion?" The NCO pointed down the road and said, "Head down there about a half mile and turn right. That's Taji. The battalion HQ is about another half mile past the turn." *No problem*, I thought.

I led my convoy triumphantly down the road then ran into another problem—there were two roads within twenty feet of each other on either side of a ditch. Which one to take? I took the nearest road on the south side of the ditch—big mistake. As I drove down this road, I began to realize my mistake. The road narrowed, and I could see the battalion HQ on the other side of the ditch. I had to turn around somehow, but the road wouldn't allow for it, as I had a significant amount of larger ammunition haulers that required a city block in order to turn around.

I crept along the ditch, hoping I'd find a solution to my dilemma. I finally got out and told the men in the vehicle behind me to wait for a bit until I found a place to turn around. As my vehicle was smaller than theirs, I figured I could make it faster. The ammo truck's wheels were hanging over the edge of the road about two inches at this point. Fortunately, about two hundred yards down the road, I found a turnoff into an Iraqi yard. I thought there was just enough room to turn the vehicles into it then back them out and turn the opposite way. I reckon a smarter fella would have backed the vehicles out the way we'd come in, but I didn't. We executed the difficult fifteen-point turn for all the vehicles, and about three hours later, I had my convoy turned the correct way.

I went back the way I had come and made the correct series of turns and finally called in "release point" (RP)[59]. I reported to the HHB

---

59 To "RP" means the maneuvering element has completed is movement and it is released to maneuver however it needs to position itself within the perimeter. It can also mean "return point" meaning I have returned to the point where I started maneuvering. Both are acceptable definitions of the terms depending on the context.

commander and asked him if he knew where I should lead my convoy. He gave me directions, and I set about delivering my convoy to their individual sections.

All in all the convoy took about seventy-two hours. We had traveled close to six hundred miles at about thirty miles an hour (the maximum speed). There were times when we had slowed to a crawl, but we made it.

We stayed in Taji for about six weeks. During this time my battalion cleared[60] the entire base. I'm still amazed at the amount of equipment I saw there. There were about twenty to thirty huge warehouses each about 150 meters by seventy-five meters filled to the top with any kind of equipment a growing army would need, from bullet-resistant plate armor to uniforms to bore bushes, etc. It was a good thing we'd found this place, because we didn't get our first push of supplies for about eight weeks.

---

60. Clearing an area in this context means to go from building to building, room to room, looking in every conceivable crevice looking for the enemy or any little nasty surprises the enemy might of left behind like a little booby traps or pitfalls intended on killing, injuring or otherwise disrupting operations.